WHAT THE DEAD HAVE
TAUGHT ME ABOUT
LIVING WELL

What the DEAD have taught me about LIVING WELL

Rebecca Rosen

Bestselling author of *Spirited* and *Awaken the Spirit Within*

with Samantha Rose

RODALE.

Mention of specific companies, organizations, or authorities in this book does not imply endorsement by the author or publisher, nor does mention of specific companies, organizations, or authorities imply that they endorse this book, its author, or the publisher.

Internet addresses and telephone numbers given in this book were accurate at the time it went to press.

Names and identifying details of people described in the book have been changed to protect the privacy of the individuals.

© 2017 by Rebecca Rosen Enterprises

All rights reserved. No part of this publication may be reproduced or transmitted in any form or by any means, electronic or mechanical, including photocopying, recording, or any other information storage and retrieval system, without the written permission of the publisher.

Rodale books may be purchased for business or promotional use or for special sales. For information, please write to:

Special Markets Department, Rodale Inc., 733 Third Avenue, New York, NY 10017

Printed in the United States of America

Rodale Inc. makes every effort to use acid-free ∞, recycled paper ♻.

Book design by Christina Gaugler

Library of Congress Cataloging-in-Publication Data is on file with the publisher.

ISBN 978-1-62336-781-7 trade hardcover

Distributed to the trade by Macmillan

2 4 6 8 10 9 7 5 3 1 hardcover

To my earth angel, Haven
You are living proof that every day holds a possibility of a miracle!

———◆———

And for Christian
Thank you for always keeping love on top and for being my rock and the
great love of my life!

CONTENTS

INTRODUCTION: YOUR LIFE IS GUIDED FROM BEYOND • ix

HOW TO APPLY THIS BOOK TO YOUR REAL LIFE • xv

MEET YOUR GUIDES • xvii

Chapter 1—Line It Up................................1

Chapter 2—Labor of Love.........................17

Chapter 3—Release Your Spiritual Weight..........37

Chapter 4—Abundance in All Things...............59

Chapter 5—Reconnect............................81

Chapter 6—Your Ground Crew.....................93

Chapter 7—Little Angels.........................113

Chapter 8—Love on Top.........................135

Chapter 9—Full Circle...........................161

EPILOGUE—LIFE IS BEAUTIFUL: H(E)AVEN IS WITHIN • 181

SIGNS FROM BEYOND • 187

SPIRITUAL TOOLS • 191

ACKNOWLEDGMENTS • 195

INDEX • 201

INTRODUCTION
Your Life Is Guided from Beyond

You're not alone.
That's what the dead whisper in my ear every day.

As a spiritual medium who has made it my life's professional work to connect the living with those who have departed this earth, I've spent the past two decades on a wondrous and amazing journey speaking to individuals, intimate groups, and large stadium audiences of men and women like you seeking insight, inspiration, and answers to life's biggest inquiries. As you would imagine, I encounter a lot of curiosity around death, heaven, and the afterlife, but interestingly, the question I continue to get asked most often is: Are my deceased loved ones still present with me in some way?

I answer this question with an unequivocal and jubilant YES. What's more, your passed loved ones surround you *every day*. Where our bodies die, our spirits do not. They continue to live on, transcending time and space, and while you may desperately miss, grieve, and long for your loved one's physical presence here on earth, your connection to them is not lost, nor will it ever be. Your relationship to them is eternal, and, whether in the physical form or in spirit, no one has a clearer connection to them than you do.

I say this with absolute confidence because every day I recognize their light and bright energetic bodies as they bounce back over from the Other Side, eager to connect with the living and assure us that death is not the end. *I am still with you. I love you. One day, we will be together again,* they say. I see them place their etheric hands on the hearts of their loved ones in an effort to alleviate suffering, loneliness, and pain. I feel them surround the living with their healing energy, and sometimes I can hear them as they quietly enter a room. And while you may not sense their subtle presence or be consciously aware of it, that doesn't mean they aren't there. Our departed loved ones are closely tuned into us. They dial in to our heartfelt emotions; often, just thinking of them draws them to our side with a readiness to provide us with comfort, clarity, protection, and answers in the here and now.

It's natural to be skeptical of what you cannot see. And even if you already believe or have a subtle feeling or strong hunch that your departed loved ones are never truly gone, you may still wonder: How can I really be sure that they are with me in some shape or form? How do I know I'm not making it fit? Or making it up? Some of you have asked me pointedly: How do you, Rebecca, know that *you're* not making it up?

I've asked myself that same question many times over the years.

When I first sat down to write this book, I resisted sharing my personal experiences of what it's like to live surrounded by spiritual guidance every day and, essentially, be *me*. I've always maintained that the mediumship work I do isn't about my life; it's about you. I believe that most authentic and accurate mediums remove themselves—their personal history, opinions, and motivations—from the messages they deliver. To avoid miscommunication or misinterpretation of the signs from beyond, it is crucial that the medium simply act as a conduit, a pure channel between the living and the dead. For as long as I've done this work, I've tried to keep myself out of the spotlight and empower you to connect with the departed on your own.

So I could simply tell you to suspend your doubts or any disbelief you may have about the existence of an afterlife. I could say that when you just *believe*, that's when you'll begin to receive and even feel the presence of the departed right alongside you. But I get it. You want proof that your loved ones are still with you and that there is something bigger beyond your day-to-day reality, and you're looking to me to give it to you.

Fair enough. And much deserved.

I believe that in addition to it being my life's work and purpose to connect the living with the dead and pass on messages of support from beyond, it's also my responsibility to share what I've witnessed and personally experienced. I want you to know what *I* know about the afterlife, to not only indulge your curiosity or comfort you and assuage your grief but also to help you understand and appreciate your day-to-day life's circumstances and challenges in the context of a much bigger picture. Throughout the following pages, I will share how I intuitively tune in to see, hear, and feel the presence of my departed loved ones, personal spirit guides, healing masters, and angelic helpers and how I use this insight to help me make better sense of, and find deeper meaning in, my world today.

Sounds kind of magical, doesn't it? My life does often feel enchanted in some kind of way, but please understand before you dive in that even though I have access to the Other Side, I'm not immune to all that this life serves up. I'm human after all—a full-time working mom and stepmom with limited time, patience, and energy. On any given day, I easily get caught up in the demands of work and family life, anxiety over money, struggles over body image, friendship drama—and there's not a week that goes by when I don't have a scheduling conflict with my babysitter and three loads of laundry waiting to be washed. Just like everyone I meet and know, I too have real-world frustrations, and while I strive every day to keep it together and be the best that I can be, the daily grind can feel overwhelming and confusing. It's not unusual for me to wake up in the morning cloudy and unclear, racking my brain for answers. In other words, even I get stuck.

This is when it is so valuable to be able to remind myself that I am not alone. A spiritual support system, what I refer to as my Team Spirit, is there to guide, comfort, and protect me through life's ups and downs. Over the years, I've relied on this support system to help me make solid and irrefutable connections for thousands of men and women desperately seeking answers, resolution, and validation that there is life after death.

At a recent large audience reading in Denver, I was speaking to a man who I sensed had a strong paternal energy standing behind him.

"I think this is your father," I said. "Why is he showing me a wallet and pointing to his pocket?"

Spirits will often show me meaningful objects like a piece of jewelry, a baby blanket, or a photograph that might help me locate their living loved one in a group or crowd. More often than not, this special object will be with the person I'm reading but hidden from view. I can't recount how many times I've mentioned a special token like this, and someone in the group will pull it out of their pocket or purse and hold it up for me to see.

"I don't know." The man shrugged his shoulders, searching for an explanation.

"Do you have something of Dad's in *your* pocket?"

"No," he said apologetically.

"Hmmmm," I said, "then maybe this message isn't for you. Let's see if I can find the rightful owner." I moved on to others in the audience.

I didn't make a match that night, but the following day, I received this e-mail:

"Rebecca, I'm the guy with the father who came through a couple of times. You asked me if I was carrying my father's wallet, and I said no. Then you asked if I had something of his in my pocket because he continued to point at his pocket. Again, I said no.

"Well, when I got home from your reading last night, it hit me like a ton of bricks! Three days before the reading, I was at dinner at P.F. Chang's, and when I finished dinner the waiter handed out fortune cookies. Honestly, my fortune said, 'A joyous reunion with a loved one will be yours within the month.' I knew I was going to your reading a few days later, so I said to myself: Dad, please give me a sign that you are with me by acknowledging this fortune. I really need some type of validation. Then I stuck it in my *wallet* and forgot about it. I have it in front of me right now, and you've made me a complete believer!"

I know that the guidance I get from the Other Side is about as dependable as it gets, so I rely on this same spiritual support system when I have nagging questions or a sense of restlessness about my own life. On any given day, I call on my Team Spirit to send me signs, provide me with insights, and line up synchronistic events throughout my day to help support and guide me in the best direction forward. Just like you, I need reassurance, and on days when nothing seems to be going in the right direction, I ask for clarity and help.

I have learned that when I take just a few focused moments to ask for higher guidance and then open up to receive it, I experience a miraculous shift in my perception, my energy level, and my mood. I am better able to calm my busy mind, make confident decisions, and release stuck hurt and grief. Sometimes I will be overcome with a swelling of forgiveness, compassion, and gratitude. In other moments, I'm simply inspired to laugh more and extend love and kindness to everyone in my life.

I believe that the only difference between a day that feels off, frustrating, or foggy and one that feels like it's unfolding easily and according to plan comes down to my connection with the Other Side. When I humbly ask for and trust in Spirit's guidance, I experience tremendous clarity and comfort. This infinite wellspring of support has a way of holding me when I'm feeling unsteady and has the power to shed light on the pieces of my life I cannot always clearly see. What I've come to understand is that we don't need to sit in temple or church, go to the grave, or be in formal meditation to have a spiritual or religious experience. The place we sit in physically isn't important; rather, the energetic space we reside in—that is, our state of mind and heart—is where we connect to Spirit.

In this book, I will take you through a day in my life and show you how my Team Spirit guides me through. Whether it's making a big life decision, coping with insecurity, or juggling my schedule as a businesswoman, wife, and mother, I turn toward my guides all the time to help me do my best moment by moment. You can do this, too, and I want to help you learn how.

I've served as a medium between this world and the next for more than two decades. After sensing and witnessing its magnificence, and also lifting the veil for countless others who have directly received life-changing messages and guidance from beyond, what I know to be absolute truth is that we each are surrounded and supported by a team of spiritual beings, the most generous forces of love and light, wherever we go. These beings intervene in your life *every day* in a variety of ways to let you know that your real-life hardships, challenges, and struggles have a rhyme, a reason, and a purpose. You're not alone to figure it all out. Whether you've ever felt the presence of these loving beings or not, they're with you. Holding, supporting, and guiding you. Right now.

That you've picked up this book means you've already opened your heart to this knowing. Perhaps you have felt their presence—either consciously or unconsciously—and it's very likely that your "team" has played a hand in guiding you here. Take a moment now to acknowledge your departed loved ones, angels, and guides and recognize that they have a plan for you. Thank them for bringing us together at this time and in this place and space. It was intentional, deliberate, and not at all coincidental.

We are intertwined on this journey together now (at least for the next 197 pages). During our time together, it will be my honor to share with you my personal stories and unseen world insight, and to also empower you with a variety of practices and tools—the very ones I rely on every day to heighten my spiritual sensitivity and receive divine inspiration. While I've learned how to channel my spiritual gifts into a 9-to-5 profession, at the end of the day, I'm really no different or more special than you. You, too, have it within you to connect with Spirit and recognize messages and signs from beyond. Take my hand. Let's step into the unknown where I'll show you how guidance from beyond shapes my daily life so that you, too, can similarly learn to live fearlessly and fully in the here and now.

HOW TO APPLY THIS BOOK TO YOUR REAL LIFE

Throughout the chapters ahead, you will be invited to many **Family Reunions,** stories where I recount how I connected clients to departed loved ones who helped them to experience clarity in their lives where there wasn't before and to "see the light," so to speak, regarding everyday struggles. My hope is that these stories help you put events, people, and situations in your life into a larger perspective.

In each chapter, I will provide you with **How I Use This in My Life,** specific examples of how I use insights and guidance from beyond to help transition from feeling stuck, unclear, and perhaps hopeless to feeling more certainty, more courageous and empowered.

I will also share **My Favorite Tools** that I use to connect with my own departed loved ones, spirit guides, and angelic helpers. Whether it's my favorite smudge spray or prayer beads, I'll explain how I use these spiritual tools in my everyday life and how they are also available to you.

Finally, I share how **Signs from the Other Side** show up in my own and my client's lives and how you can similarly learn to recognize the signs of your departed loved ones and guides "talking" to you, and how to interpret and relate these signs to your life.

MEET YOUR GUIDES

Every day, you are surrounded by your own Team Spirit—departed loved ones, personal guides, and angelic helpers and healers. As you read through the pages ahead, these loving and enlightened spirits will likely begin to make contact with you and provide you with spiritual guidance (if they haven't already), so let's spend a minute here on who and what these spirits are.

First and foremost, your departed loved ones. You know who they are. Most of the time, the departed reach out simply to say hello, lighten your pain, and wrap their etheric arms around you. They surround you in this way to remind you that they're never truly gone. They are ever-present in spirit. For many years after his death, my dad made his presence known. While at first, he came through with simple messages—*I am still with you. I love you*—he now guides me from beyond to help survivors of tragic deaths like suicide. I understand this specific need for closure and peace because I'm a survivor myself. Both my grandmother and father took their own lives.

Along with our departed loved ones, we are each supported by spirit guides. These loving spirits often work in partnership with your departed loved ones, but are typically spirits of people you haven't known in your lifetime. Our guides are enlightened spirits who have "been there, done that"—meaning they were once human and now they're between lifetimes, taking a break from physical life and working from the Other Side to guide the living. Your spirit guides (you'll have many throughout your lifetime) gravitate to you from beyond, based on your similar personalities, interests, challenges, and life stories. Different guides cross over at different times to help you learn and grow, depending on the level and type of support you need at any given moment. I often refer to spirit guides being "on assignment" with the living.

I'm currently being supported by several guides, including one who calls herself Sash. She's shown me in meditation that her assignment is to help keep my spiritual energy clean and fluid, which is imperative for the work that I do.

I sense her guidance when I feel suddenly compelled to get outside in nature, make an appointment for a massage, or take a long bath at the end of the night—all activities that soothe and bring balance back to my energetic body.

We all also have guides on assignment with us to work in a less abstract way by helping us through more practical points in our lives—dealing with divorce, surviving the first year of motherhood, managing a career change, or dealing with sickness or a death in the family. In these instances, your visiting guides may inspire you to move in a particular direction or make a difficult decision, or simply surround you so you feel supported and less alone.

Finally, while your visiting guides come and go throughout your lifetime, your guardian guide (more often referred to as your guardian angel) has been with you from the day you were born and will guide and protect you until your last breath. Your guardian acts primarily as your advocate and protector, guiding you gently through life, and has the ability to intervene and assist you when your life depends on it. My guardian calls herself Maya, and she has been in the background of my life for as long as I can remember. Maya most often visits me in dreams to help me sort through an emotional struggle or dilemma. Our guardian guides feel everything we're feeling, and their loving guidance is delivered through our emotions more than our physical senses.

Departed loved ones, spirit guides, and guardian angels. That's a lot of support, wouldn't you agree?

Most people go through their lives unaware of this spiritual support and guidance, but your "team" is on the ready and available to you as soon as you ask for their insight and assistance. And once you do, it's just a matter of time and practice before you begin to sense, hear, and recognize their presence in your life. Your departed loved ones and spirit guides send you dozens of messages and signs throughout every day, but like background music that's always on, you won't necessarily notice them until you turn down everything else.

As you read through my day-in-a-life story, I hope you begin to see that the more often you ask for guidance and remain open to receive it, the stronger your connection with Spirit will become.

For a self-guided meditation to meet your departed loved ones and spirit guides and begin sensing the "signs," go to rebeccarosen.com/connecting -signs-meditation and download the free audio file.

CHAPTER 1

LINE IT UP

I've served as a spiritual medium for more than twenty years, communicating healing and often life-changing messages from the dead to the living, and in that time I've learned the difference between a dream and a spirit visitation. A dream is fleeting. While you may wake up remembering pieces of it, it usually fades quite quickly. But a spirit visitation is unshakable. It can feel just as real as an actual encounter, and the memory of it stays with you long afterward, if not forever.

What woke me up this morning was definitely the latter. I sat up in bed feeling that the spirit of a baby girl was in the room. I'd become aware of her presence off and on over the past two weeks, often waking me up in the dead of night where I'd experience a strong sense that she was right beside me. This morning, she'd startled me awake. I felt a mental tug in my sleep, as if she were dragging me out of a dream. *Pay attention to me*, she whispered. My eyes scanned the still-dark bedroom for a streak or orb of light, which is how I commonly see spirits. She remained elusive. "Who are you, baby girl?" I wasn't afraid. I could feel that she was a loving spirit. Where I couldn't identify who this child was, I knew with absolute certainty that I was being contacted from the Other Side.

Early morning wake-up calls like these are not uncommon for me. Departed souls hoping to connect with their living loved ones often show up on my mental doorstep, so to speak, before I've even had my first cup of coffee. Sometimes they'll nudge me awake, pressing me with their special energy until I pay attention to them. Other times they may quietly drop into that groggy space between sleeping and waking, the perfect doorway between this world and the next. When our waking minds are quiet and our physical bodies are still, the door to our unconscious mind opens, and in this place of wide, empty space, the dead reach out across the divide where they hope to meet us halfway between their world and ours. Spirits may use this time to simply say hello and let us know they are still present in our lives. Other times the departed have more important information that they want to impress into our minds before the sun comes up. The mornings you wake up with sudden clarity or an inspired idea, you probably have someone on the Other Side to thank.

In between sleep and waking, we're more receptive to hearing, seeing, and feeling the presence of spirits who have left this world for the next. As a natural medium, I'm especially open. Spirits will flood my senses in a variety of ways—through my heightened sense of sight, sound, feeling, and intuitive knowing.

When I first began communicating with the Other Side, I relied on my clairaudience—the ability we all have to hear the dead. On one unremarkable day in 1997 while sitting in a bookstore, I felt a strong urge to sit down and write in my journal. As soon as I found the nearest chair and turned to a blank page, words began to pour out of me and through my pen. It was as if I were transcribing a conversation that I was hearing inside my head. My hand felt to be involuntarily pulled back and forth across the page, and it became startlingly clear that the words, short sentences, and phrases were not mine but of my deceased grandmother. She whispered clearly in my ear, *I'm here for you.*

I wrote about this experience extensively in my first book, *Spirited.* When Grandma Babe first made her presence known to me through this process of channeling spirits called automatic writing, I was a young college student struggling with depression and an unconscious and very unhealthy sleep-eating disorder. Therapy, various medications, and loving support from family and friends hadn't helped me out of my dangerous low, and I felt desperately at my end—hopeless, reckless, and utterly alone. It was at this pivotal moment when my grandmother reached out from the Other Side to take my hand and gently guide me toward the healing I was crying out for.

Over the course of the next year and a half, Grandma Babe helped me to develop my spiritual gifts and spoke to me most often through my heightened clairaudience—the ability to hear the dead. I interpreted her words and guidance through my pen, and she passed onto the page details I'd never known about her own life struggle with depression, including revelations about her tragic suicide. She encouraged me to take a different path, and her ever presence and loving support served to save my life. This experience proved to me how our lives can magically turn around when we awaken to and accept guidance from beyond.

Since learning how to connect through my sense of clear hearing, I've heightened all my intuitive and psychic senses to receive messages from beyond. While we've all got them, my innate senses are more turned on, kind of like a 1,000-watt bulb without a dimmer function. Sometimes my feelings and auditory and visual impressions are faint and easy to dismiss, while other times the messages I receive are crystal clear. For example, it's not unusual for me to feel intense ringing in my ears when a spirit wants to speak through my clairaudience. They literally call me until I pick up. When a spirit taps into my clairsentience, or clear sense, I'm often flooded with strong emotions like grief, guilt, shame, or regret around an unresolved situation that is still hurting a living loved one or holding that person back from fully enjoying or moving forward with their life. Other times I will sense Spirit on a physical level. A bodily sensation might take over me, like feeling release and relief in my muscles. Sometimes I will get the chills or feel as if someone has lightly brushed up against me.

How I sense or feel the departed really depends on the unique spirit coming through and what he or she wants me to know. For example, when I'm overcome with a feeling of intense pressure in the chest, I can be pretty sure that the spirit died from a heart attack. A tightening around my throat typically means that the spirit had difficulty breathing at the end of his or her life. And if I feel a quick, sharp pinch or a jolt in my body as if I've had the wind knocked out of me, I know that the spirit experienced some kind of sudden impact before dying, like in a car accident or from a fall.

This morning it was my clairsentience that kicked in. The spirit of the baby girl *felt* near. Her soft, angelic presence sent a tingle up my back. The fact that she'd made contact with me four, five, or was it six times now meant that she was powerful in addition to being persistent. It takes a tremendous amount of energy for a spirit to cross over into our physical world. Our world is heavy and energetically dense, while the spirit world is light, airy, and buzzing at lightning speed. This makes it virtually invisible to human eyes, and yet this unseen world is very close.

While our most celebrated and iconic images of the afterlife and heaven are of an untouchable world high above us, what spirits have shown me is that the Other Side actually surrounds us on all sides. It's right in front, beside, and around us. Still, it can be compared to a powerful force field, and breaking through isn't easy. For a spirit to cross this energetic barrier requires tremendous focus and practice, as well as a strong determination to do so. And once they've crossed back over to the physical world, they can typically only visit for a short time before they disappear. In readings, I refer to this as a spirit "pulling their energy back": They never truly vanish; they simply readjust to a higher vibrational frequency that is invisible to the human eye.

When the spirit of the baby girl pulled back, I had the sensation of a cool ocean tide receding off of my toes until I could no longer feel her. "You'll return," I thought to myself. If I've learned anything as a medium, it's that you can't force an introduction. Spirits reveal themselves in their own time and unique way, and when they want to be known and heard, they'll find a way to do it. I sat further up in bed, trusting that when she was ready, she'd fully reveal herself and her message to me.

FAMILY REUNIONS

Making Introductions

It was while I was doing a group reading of more than five hundred people in Los Angeles that I saw a visible spark of light directly behind a man in the audience. I clairaudiently heard the name Jeffrey repeated in my head and said directly to him, "I have a message for Jeffrey. Is this for you?" He looked completely caught off guard, and turned to the man sitting next to him who offered, "Yes, his name is

Jeffrey, but he's not a believer. He's my buddy, and I dragged him here tonight."

The spirits of grandparents will often appear directly behind their living grandchildren, with the maternal grandparent often appearing on the left and the paternal on the right. The light behind Jeffrey was on the left side, so I said to him, "I feel strongly the presence of your maternal grandfather in the room. I'm also hearing the name Albert repeated over and over in my head. Was your grandfather's name Albert?" Spirits love to name-drop, and will frequently project into my consciousness their first and last names to help identify them.

"No," Jeffrey shook his head. "His name was James."

I continued, "Well, this spirit is clearly saying Martin and Albert, both names together. Do either of these names mean anything to you?" He shook his head again.

This was puzzling to me because each time I said the names together, Martin Albert, I saw a bright flash of light behind Jeffrey. Whenever I see a flash or burst of light behind the person I'm reading, it's as if the spirit is underlining, in effect validating, what I'm saying in the moment. This tells me that I'm accurately interpreting the messages and the signs. But Jeffrey wasn't so believing. In fact, he looked at me like most skeptics do—like I was crazy. So after several more attempts to connect the dots for him, I moved on to someone else in the audience.

I felt somewhat frustrated that I hadn't made a solid connection for Jeffrey, but I quickly let it go. What I've learned, because I've experienced it so many times, is that what doesn't initially click or make sense for the person I'm reading will often become clear later on. The reasons for this vary, but typically one of three things is happening: The person I'm reading feels put on the spot and goes blank; the details I've passed on haven't unfolded yet, so it doesn't add up in the moment; or the recipient has no knowledge of the information I've passed on, and it has to be validated by someone else.

So I wasn't too surprised when Jeffrey called me at my office the following day to tell me what had unfolded after he'd gone home and recounted the reading to his mother. When he told her that I'd repeated the names Martin and Albert, her jaw dropped to the floor. She quickly pulled open her desk drawer and fumbled around until she found what she was looking for. She handed her son a piece of paper. "This is your grandfather's birth certificate," she said. "He emigrated from Europe before I was born and changed his name before arriving in this country. To all of us, Grandpa was always James Elliot, but that's not his birth name." Her hand shook as she pointed at the document. Jeffrey looked down at the name on the birth certificate: Albert Martin. That's when his jaw hit the floor, too.

The proof that I'm communicating with the spirit world usually comes with an aha moment or a surprise like this. Spirits will provide me with irrefutable names, dates, and sometimes very obscure and seemingly insignificant details to prove to their living loved ones that they're right there with them.

"What kind of surprise do you have in store for me?" I wondered about the spirit of the baby girl who'd woken me up. Perhaps she would appear later today and make her presence known. I had a full schedule of readings at the office, so it was entirely likely she'd show up again. With that, I made a mental note to keep my eyes wide open as I slid out of bed.

SET THE INTENTION

In my household of seven that includes my husband, Chris, and the five kids between us—two from my previous marriage and three from his—mornings can accelerate to one hundred miles an hour, and *fast*. For me to do the focused mediumship work I will do throughout the day, and to also just be a calm and kind person to my family and those around me, it's imperative that I get ahead of life's momentum before I get run over. The best way I know to do this is to sit for a few quiet moments at the start of my day and "line it up." This is my own expression for setting a clear intention, or hope, for my day ahead and asking to be connected, protected, guided, and directed from beyond. I've found that my days flow much more easily when I acknowledge right off the bat that I may need extra help and then unapologetically ask for it.

Our departed loved ones and guides are always available to help shed light on our daily lives, which is exactly why I make a practice of asking for their guidance and a clear direction forward every morning. So once I've had a chance to truly wake up, and usually after Chris brings me a hot cup of coffee, I will position myself at the base of my bed where I will sit in a short meditation. I'm a big believer in meditation, the simple act of concentrating on the breath to quiet and calm the mind and become fully present in the here and now. It's when I'm present that I feel the most clear. When I don't take time first thing to meditate and "line it up," I feel noticeably unclear—foggy, fidgety, and moody.

In addition to calming my nerves and bringing me into the present moment, meditation also shifts and lifts my energy to match the higher vibration of the spirit world. Meditation is the most effective way for me to get into this kind of higher head space—I actually think it might be the only way—which is why I meditate before every individual client reading I do and sometimes for several hours when I'm preparing for a large audience.

During a deep meditation like I do before an audience reading, I may feel a sense of expansion and spaciousness, along with a physical lightness in my body. At times I've felt weightless, like I could lift off of the ground. It's when I reach this higher state, what many refer to as the Higher Self, that I meet spirits halfway between this world and the next and receive their heartfelt messages for the living. That said, I don't have to get this high, so to speak, nor do I want to first thing in the morning. When my meditation practice is solely for me, I like to keep it fairly low to the ground.

My meditation space is the first thing I see when I wake up, and I've designed it that way on purpose. It serves as an instant reminder that loving spirits are present in my daily life, and it expresses my gratitude to be connected to something bigger than myself. I've decorated a mantel that hangs along our far bedroom wall with aromatic candles and beautiful found objects that hold special significance to me. There are dimes, nails, stones—

all physical reminders and "signs" from my dad that I've found along my path at different points in my life. I've also placed special gifts from clients and friends on my altar like crystals and cards, and in the center sit a cluster of statues of my favorite archangels and ascended masters like Buddha, Ganesh, Lakshmi, and Quan Yin.

Above my meditation space hangs an intention board of inspiring pictures and words, something I create every December as I head into the new year to remind me what I want more of in my life.

ONE OF MY FAVORITE TOOLS

A Meditation Space

Many of us are used to seeing altars in houses of worship, but have you ever considered creating a special space like this in other areas of your life? A dedicated meditation space in your home can be your go-to spot to quiet your mind and set the daily intention to invite in more clarity and guidance from beyond. When you focus your attention—in other words, your love, thoughts, and prayers—on a space like this, your departed loved ones and guides are drawn to it. They feel your focused energy, and it draws them closer.

CLEAR THE SPACE

Select a special area in your home or office like a side table, a bookcase, or a mantel. Ideally, this space is one you pass by frequently, which will remind you to take time each day to connect with your departed loved ones and your guides.

SELECT SPECIAL ITEMS

To decorate your special space, choose items that you feel positively connected to, that hold significant meaning to you, and that also remind you of your departed loved ones. In readings, spirits will often make mention of specific objects that memorialize them.

If particular deities, teachers, or angels resonate with you, consider placing a picture or statue of them next to the other objects, as well. These may change over time. Lately, I've been feeling especially drawn to Quan Yin, the goddess of mercy and compassion. She's come to me in many meditations, telling me she's working with and through me to help serve others, as a messenger of love, peace, and truth, so I have placed a few big and small statues of her on my altar. When considering what to put in your space, select items that feel beautiful, inspired, and inviting to *you*.

ARRANGE

Arranging the objects you've chosen is an important part of making this space yours. I suggest you do less thinking and more *feeling* when arranging. In other words, allow yourself to be guided. I will sit in front of my meditation space and ask Spirit to show me or inspire me as to where to place each item. It's kind of like intuitively directed feng shui. Once my special objects are in place and the arrangement feels right, I set the intention to experience the connections I seek.

A DAILY PRACTICE

My meditation practice is pretty simple: I close my eyes and focus on the inhale and exhale of my breath, and allow any and all thoughts to come and go. On days when I find it especially hard to quiet my mind, I may use a mantra like "be still and know" and repeat it over and over again until my mental turbulence becomes still. In that open space I set my intention for the day. Setting an intention is not unlike saying a morning prayer, and I keep mine straightforward.

This particular morning, I repeated: "God, guides, and departed loved ones: Let my day flow easily. Help to clear obstacles out of my way. Lead me where I need to go and where I'm needed most."

As I said this, I clairvoyantly saw my guides holding out their hands to lead me, along with a mental flash of an open road ahead of me and an illuminated center divider line pulling me in a clear direction forward. With my eyes still closed and imagining myself being steered forward in the direction of light, I opened and stretched out my palms. I visualized myself driving forward into a burst of white light as it enveloped me from all sides, almost like walking into a cloud.

I continued to set the intention in my mind: "God, guides, and departed loved ones: I give you my day. I let go of my need to control, and I surrender fully to you. I trust that you will guide me and that the day will unfold just as it should. I surrender to what I cannot and do not know."

It might seem counterproductive, but I often line up my day by giving up control of my day. I do this because my mediumship work continues to show me over and over again that we each only have a limited amount of control over our lives.

As I continued to sit in meditation, imagining myself enveloped in protective, white light, I told myself, "Have faith in the bigger plan coming together behind the scenes."

Again, having faith when there's no clear reason to have it is hard for anyone. But the guidance I receive from the Other Side is to trust and just *let it be*. I cannot tell you how many times I've been struggling over the earthly details of how, where, or when a particular situation will unfold when I turn on the radio or walk into a coffee shop and the Beatles song "Let It Be" is playing overhead. A clear sign from Spirit!

Signs from the Other Side: LET IT BE

I once had a reading with a young man named Ryan whose mom had died a few years earlier of cancer. Her spirit barreled through from the Other Side, making me *feel* intense anxiety, almost like I was having a panic attack. Then she flashed in my mind an image of my first part-time job at the Gap. My boss was a family friend, and she'd helped me get a sales clerk position, but it was clear to me pretty quickly that the job wasn't a good fit for me. I only lasted the summer before I respectfully quit. I understood that Ryan's mother in spirit was using this personal experience to draw a parallel to her son. I asked Ryan if he was struggling at his place of employment. He confirmed that he was battling severe anxiety and had considered leaving his job. Ryan's mother clairvoyantly showed me a big yellow light, my sign for caution—to pause and look deeper into a decision or situation before moving forward.

"Your mom is impressing me with her desire for you to stay where you're at. Even though it may feel uncomfortable or like a dead end, there's more learning and growing to be done here before moving on to the next thing. She's saying that she will be by your side every step of the way, and she's showing me a bumblebee and a birthday cake. Does this mean anything to you?"

Ryan looked stunned and then told me that he'd recently suffered the first bee sting of his life on his twenty-first birthday. I smiled. "Your mom was behind this. She sent you the bee on your birthday as a message to 'just be.' Stay the course and have faith that your life will unfold as it should and Mom will be with you to guide you along."

THE ASK

Every morning, after I've set my intention for the day to flow easily and I've surrendered the details of how it will exactly play out, I ask my departed loved ones and guides to support me throughout the day by sending me signs either of their presence or to validate my choices, decisions, and movement forward. I will often ask them out loud and point-blank, "Is there anything you want me to know?"

While our departed loved ones and spirit guides feel us and hear our thoughts and requests for help and guidance, they will not interfere until you invite them in. You must first ask for their guidance, and then you must open yourself up to all possibilities. Guidance and signs from beyond show up in many different ways—through dreams, music, found objects, threads of conversation, and even inspired thoughts. Because of the many varied ways spirits attempt to get our attention, it's imperative you let go of any preconceived ideas of what guidance from beyond looks like. Our minds naturally love to talk us out of things we don't quite understand, but my advice is to be receptive to whatever shows up and trust that you'll know it when you see it.

Signs from the Other Side: YOU'LL KNOW IT WHEN YOU SEE IT

In a reading with another young man named Chase, his deceased aunt came through from the Other Side, reassuring him that he would go to college. She used my own frame of reference to tell me this by flashing in my mind a mental movie of the day I graduated from the University of Florida. But Chase shook his head regretfully and relayed to me a conversation he'd recently had with his parents—they didn't have the money to send him to school as they had always planned.

I said, "Your aunt is showing me dollar bills and saying that there is enough money, and she's handing it to you as a gift. She wants you to know that she will take care of you around this and she is proud of you for wanting to get a higher education."

Chase appreciated the message but couldn't imagine where the money would come from. He made an off-hand joke, "Is Aunt Jan going to drop dollar bills from heaven?"

I told him, "Be open to the signs in the next few days. I feel strongly that your aunt has something up her sleeve."

Well, two nights later, Chase had a vivid dream where his aunt showed him an envelope hidden on a shelf in his living grandmother's closet (his aunt's sister) and that he should go find it. The next morning, when Chase couldn't shake the dream, he went over to his grandmother's house and told her about the dream. She was intrigued, so together they went looking for the envelope. After much digging around, they found a dusty manila envelope at the top of the guest room closet. It was stuffed with balance sheets of stocks and bonds that Aunt Jan had invested in for years—and sure enough, Chase was named as the sole beneficiary on the accounts. The available funds would pay for his entire four-year education!

Signs like this from beyond are thrilling to receive, but in my opinion, one of the more magical ways spirits talk to the living is by creating synchronistic events in our everyday lives. C. G. Jung coined this term when his book *Synchronicity: An Acausal Connecting Principle* was published in 1952. He described synchronicity as "meaningful coincidence" or meaningful sequences of unusual, accidental events that hold a subjective meaning to the person involved. In other words, you recognize synchronicity when it happens—they're those head-scratching moments where everything seems to line up in a perfectly weird and magical way. And yet what I understand from my regular glimpses of the bigger picture is that there's really nothing weird about them because there really are no accidents or coincidences!

In readings, spirits are so often excited to reveal that each of our lives has a plan, an order, and a grand design, and they take great pleasure in orchestrating synchronistic events in our lives, as if to say, "See—I told you so! Let go, let it be, trust in the flow." My deceased father, Shelly, one of my biggest advocates and helpers from the Other Side, regularly makes his presence known in my day-to-day life in a number of synchronistic ways, most notably by dropping Iowa Hawkeyes paraphernalia in my path. My dad went to the University of Iowa, and he spent his life as a devout Hawkeye. Also, later in his life, when he experienced his own spiritual awakening, Dad identified the "hawk" as a sign from his guides (whenever he saw one, he felt protected and directed from beyond). It wasn't until years after death that I put it all together: Dad was using the Hawkeye logo as his sign to me. Hawkeyes ball caps, bumper stickers, and T-shirts would somehow cross my path when I was thinking intently about Dad or asking him to help me in some way.

On a recent trip to San Francisco for a series of small group readings, Dad pulled out all the stops to get my attention and let me know that he was with me. It started when I got to my gate at the Denver airport and without realizing it, I sat down next to a man who resembled Dad in looks and mannerisms. We struck up a conversation, and as fate would have it, he had ties to Iowa. A few hours later, after I arrived at my hotel in downtown San Francisco, a man in a Hawkeyes hoodie stepped into the elevator beside me, making it impossible not to notice the logo on his sweatshirt. An Iowa Hawkeyes fan on the West Coast—*what are the odds?*

But then things became even more synchronistic when this same man joined my intimate reading of twelve people that evening. When his deceased sister came through from the Other Side and revealed to me through words and mental pictures that her brother was struggling with debt, I understood why Dad had dropped so many signs and made his presence known—to draw a parallel between his own life and that of my client. Dad had also struggled financially. Once I put it all together, I understood how my client needed help.

People often ask me, how do I know I'm not making the signs up?

Practice.

Noticing synchronicities and reading the signs from the departed and our guides take practice. Begin by paying closer attention to all your senses— what you're feeling, sensing, hearing, and seeing moment to moment. If you're suddenly overcome with clarity, inspiration, or an overwhelming feeling of being pulled or guided in one direction or another, consider that your departed loved ones and guides are impressing you from the Other Side. If you start to notice a recurring number combination, a word or phrase, or a special symbol emerge in your morning meditation or throughout your waking days, take note. If you continue to run into the same person over and over again, or find yourself in a similar situation repeatedly, acknowledge the synchronicity. Does this person or situation have something important to teach or relay to you? Remember that the departed and your guides will not intervene in your life until you ask them to, so set aside time each day to meet them halfway by setting the intention to connect with them and then open up to receive the many ways they show up, nudge you, and speak to you.

How I Use This in My Life: **LINE IT UP**

Before you get out of bed in the morning and jump into the busyness of the hours ahead, take a few moments to "line it up" and surrender to what you cannot and do not know. Take a few slow, meditative breaths and focus on drawing white light down into your crown chakra, the middle space just above your eyes that serves as the portal between this world and the next. Imagine this light flooding in, through, and around you as you say: "God, guides, and departed loved ones: Let my day flow easily. Lead me where I need to go and where I'm needed most. I let go of my need to control, and I surrender fully to you. Thank you for making your presence known, sending me signs, guiding and protecting me each step of the way."

THIS PARTICULAR MORNING, as I asked for a sign to help direct me through the day, I felt the presence of my guides surround me as the image of a sunflower appeared in my mind's eye. I smiled at this familiar nod from beyond. Spirits frequently use sunflowers to get my attention. I was letting my mind linger on the image when my youngest son, Sam, came bursting through the door. "Mommy!"

My seven-year-old stumbled into our bedroom with dreamy eyes, pleading to climb into bed next to me. I never turn down a warm snuggle from Sam, so I laid back down in bed and wrapped my arms around him. I'd probably only sat in meditation for a total of five minutes, but that's better than nothing. I had set a clear intention for my day to flow easily and on purpose, and now I was mentally ready to shift my focus from the unseen world toward the very real world of getting five kids, plus myself, dressed and out the door on time. As Sam and I lay cuddled together for a minute longer, I heard my cellphone vibrate on my nightstand.

"Mommy, your phone," he reached out and handed it to me.

It was a text from my good friend Janie. It said: "She's here! My niece came in the middle of the night." She'd attached an adorable photo of a new-born baby girl in the delivery room.

Looking at her, I couldn't help but draw a parallel between this baby and the spirit who had nudged me awake. They weren't one and the same; I knew that. This one was in a chunky new body, and the other was still in spirit form. *Who are you?* I wondered again.

CHAPTER 2

LABOR OF LOVE

I dropped Jakob and Sam off at school. They immediately tore off toward the playground where several of their friends were playing four square. "Don't forget your backpacks," I called after them. Brian, their dad, would be picking them up from school, and I wouldn't see them for a few days. It's always with a mixture of sadness and a pang of guilt when I pack them up for a few days away at "Dad's house." My kids now live a split life, and my heart aches for all the day-to-day adjustments they've had to make since our divorce. At the same time, when their week with Brian rolls around, I tend to welcome a few days off from mommy patrol to reenergize myself and also reconnect with Chris. If I'm being perfectly honest, our five kids between us are *a lot*.

Throughout our many years together, I referred to Brian publicly as my soul mate and credited my dead grandmother for bringing us together in this lifetime. She predicted our union from beyond, and I used to say that Brian was her gift to me, my reward for having the courage and the heart to follow my own path, to be "me" no matter what. When we divorced in 2012, I understood why many of my friends, family, and clients were shocked. Given how I'd framed our relationship as divinely orchestrated for so many years, I appreciated that our parting would be confusing. It seemed as if some people questioned the accuracy of the guidance I'd received. I wasn't surprised when people wondered, "If Brian is your 'soul mate,' why would you split up?"

Fair enough.

The answer is that Brian was and still *is* my soul mate. What spirits have shown me again and again is that most of us have more than one soul mate in our lifetime. At different points, we attract certain partners, friends, and allies into our life experience or are drawn to others whom we feel a deep closeness and connection with, based on what we need emotionally, physically, philosophically, and more importantly, spiritually, at that time. On a deep level, our soul mates serve to help us learn important life lessons and to spiritually grow—and in most cases, our time together with a soul mate was predestined. It was meant to be, in other words, even when the relationship involves conflict or eventually ends in separation. Spirits have clairvoyantly relayed this to me by showing me a cast of characters that come and go throughout our life movie. Some stay until the end, some reappear throughout, and others are only in one scene. But for however long they join you, they play a significant role.

I won't forget a concerned e-mail I received after publicly announcing my divorce: "The vow of a marriage is for a lifetime. What do the dead have to say about breaking that sacred commitment?"

What the departed have helped me understand is that every marriage and relationship we have holds significance, and yet sometimes they must end to propel us forward in life. Seen through a spiritual lens, endings are actually new beginnings that are often beneficial to both people, if not immediately then over time.

But I understand just as well as anyone who has gone through a difficult breakup or divorce how natural it is to equate endings with failure.

My mind definitely went there, when Brian and I were deciding to end our marriage. We'd struggled for many years to save it. But after spending countless hours in counseling resisting, denying, trying to control and make our relationship fit, finally my intuitive, higher guidance overruled my mind's interpretation of failure. It said, "You haven't failed. It's simply time to let go and move on. Trust that you will both heal. Have faith in what comes next."

In readings, spirits counsel their living loved ones to allow all of life, including our closest relationships, to flow and evolve. To change into *what comes next*. Brian and I spent many wonderful years helping one another grow. He came into my life when I was learning to develop my connection with the Other Side, and he wholeheartedly supported and believed in me.

His encouragement gave me the courage I needed to come out of the shadows and practice my gift openly. In many respects, I credit him for jump-starting my life's work. I similarly helped to empower him by encouraging his natural talents and strengths.

But then, over the years, Brian's needs changed and so did mine, and in order to get what we each most wished for, it became clear that we had to end our relationship and start again. As hard as it was to face this truth, we knew it was the right guidance. We explained to our boys, "Mommy's and Daddy's paths are going in different directions, but we'll always be a family."

Sometimes couples are able to change and grow within the partnership or the marriage, but in other cases this simply isn't possible because one or both have moved on to a different way of thinking or being. This is especially true when one, or both, of the partners stagnates or becomes depressed or resentful of the other person. This is when a relationship needs to shift, sometimes dramatically. Still, a split, separation, or breakup doesn't discount the time you spent together or what you learned from each other to grow in this lifetime.

This truth applies to all our relationships. Think of a person who was important in your life, but where you hit a point when you felt like you had to pause, move past or away from them in order to get to your next step. This distance likely made room for that friend, colleague, or mentor to connect with someone else, or themselves, in order for them to get to their next important step in their lives. Though ending a marriage can be far more complicated, energetically it is the same: a deeply important relationship with someone to whom you owe a duty of respect and love and loyalty, and that includes the duty of not holding one another back from moving forward.

In my experience, this only works if you mutually make the decision to end things respectfully. Respect comes in the form of putting your hurt feelings aside and doing what you believe is in the best interest for both you and your partner. Not only is this respectful, but it's an act of generosity. This is what Brian and I worked to do for one another, and our relationship and our family are better for it.

I have this clarity now, and yet the day we decided to end our marriage, I was terrified we were making a huge mistake. Even when you know you're doing the right thing, fear has a way of making you think you're doing the wrong thing. My lingering doubts were accompanied by feelings of empathy for Brian. My clairsentience kicked in big-time; I could deeply *feel* Brian's pain and sadness, and I carried the weight of both his and my grief. That's when Spirit stepped in to help strengthen our decision.

Signs from the Other Side: FOLLOW YOUR GUT

Not long after Brian moved out of our house, a woman named Rachel came to me for a reading. I immediately sensed the spirit of a mother figure standing to the right of Rachel as I heard the name "Patty" loud and clear ringing in my ears.

"Is Patty your mom?" I asked. "Is she deceased?"

"Yes," Rachel confirmed.

Patty's spirit then sent a strong current of anxiety through my body. My heart began to race. I started to feel light-headed as a memory flashed into my mind of a time when I had gotten lost hiking in Poudre Canyon, the mountains outside of Fort Collins. I drew a parallel to Rachel.

"Have you been suffering recently from panic attacks?" I asked her.

"I have," she said without hesitation, "and I call on Mom when I do."

"She hears you," I said. "And she's here now to help you."

Patty then flashed an image of Brian and me in my mind's eye, and I knew instinctively where she was going with this. I asked, "Are you questioning your marriage? I'm getting a sense that there's anxiety and conflict there."

Again, Rachel nodded and described a situation I knew well: She worried that she and her husband had outgrown their relationship. In Rachel's case, she was trying to move forward with her life, while her husband seemed to be stuck in a cycle of childhood wounds that fastened him to the past and made him unhappy in his present life. His attitude was negative and controlling, she said, and Rachel felt suffocated. Still, she stayed in the marriage because she felt obligated to keep her family together despite her mounting anxiety and dissatisfaction.

I said, "Mom is pointing at your stomach and making me feel a tightness there." Again, Patty was using my own frame of reference—I know too well what it feels like to swallow uncomfortable feelings. I've done this at various times in my life, and the result is often chronic stomach pain.

"I have GI issues," Rachel sighed.

"Your body is talking to you," I said. "Anytime you feel uneasy or sick to your stomach, it's important to check in with your 'gut' feelings. We each hold our deepest and strongest emotions in our solar plexus, the area around the navel. This is also the location of your third chakra that controls metabolism and digestion. GI issues are often the physical manifestation of unresolved or uncomfortable feelings, and this is what your mom is showing me. You may develop disease in your body if you keep stuffing down your true feelings about your marriage."

Rachel looked at me, alarmed.

"It's not necessarily *going* to happen," I assured her, "but Mom is encouraging you to speak up."

A few weeks after our reading, Rachel called to thank me for delivering the words she needed to hear. She said she'd finally found the courage to ask her husband for a separation, and since then her panic attacks had stopped. She audibly exhaled, "I feel like I can finally breathe again, and my stomach isn't in knots."

When we stay in relationships and situations out of obligation, guilt, or fear of change or feelings of loss, our departed loved ones and guides will often intervene. They may influence your thoughts, inspire you to make a change, or show you "signs" that point you in a new direction. If you look the other way, or dismiss or try and hide from their guidance, then they may turn up the dial on your uncomfortable feelings until you can no longer ignore them.

Toward the end of my marriage to Brian, I struggled with my own intuition and guidance—what I knew in my gut and my heart—for fear of sabotaging my relationship or of being alone. I know that Brian also experienced his own version of a "block," and eventually we both recognized that we had to step away from our fear and turn toward the truth. Following your heart can be costly, but it can set you free, and I believe that freedom is always worth the high price.

WORK-LIFE BALANCE

I lingered for another minute, watching Jakob and Sam on the playground before getting back in the car, when I distinctly heard one of the boys call out in a teasing voice, "You can't catch me, baby girl!" This gave me pause. *Baby girl?* Was the spirit from earlier this morning trying to get my attention *again*? It seemed like a stretch or a weird coincidence, even though I know there really are none. My cell phone rang, interrupting this thought. It was Brian.

"Hey, I was wondering if you could switch a couple days this week—take the boys again tonight through Saturday, and I'll pick them up on Sunday?"

Brian and I have a week on, week off parenting schedule. "Sure," I said. "I'll keep them tonight, but I have to work tomorrow."

"Over the weekend—again?"

He was right to question me. Saturday is typically my weekend day off with the boys, and as much as I try not to let anything interfere with our time together, sometimes I have to work. Scratch that: I make the choice to work. When the number of people requesting spiritual guidance and healing stretches beyond a normal workweek, I will sometimes add weekend hours to fit everyone in. I do this because I empathize with my clients' longing to connect with the mother, father, sibling, best friend, or child they've lost. I feel their deep desire for answers, validation, comfort, and closure, and I want to help.

But spending my off days in the unseen world means sacrificing time with those I love in this world, and I struggle to balance the two. While I feel extremely blessed for my special gift to help others and to do the healing work I do, I have days when I question my work-life balance. Is it off-kilter? Am I serving all areas of my life equally and fairly? It feels like I'm always on the go, racing from one thing to the next. My challenge is to find the balance and walk the middle way, as the wise Buddha taught.

Life is a demanding push and pull, and I don't know many women who don't struggle like I do to balance it all from day to day, whether they have full-time careers, stay at home with their children, or do something else altogether. Clients often confide that they're overworked and exhausted and have limited energy to share with their spouses, partners, children, or friends, let alone have anything left to give to themselves. Their departed loved ones and guides will often validate this by impressing me with a sense of being overwhelmed, almost like feeling suffocated, and I will clairvoyantly see a lopsided set of scales, which indicate that their living loved one is struggling to balance their life.

When I'm feeling pulled in a thousand directions, I often dream that I'm in a car that gets a flat tire or has a dead battery. Over the years, these recurring caution signs from beyond have served to remind me how important it is to slow down, recharge, and steer my life back toward the middle. When Brian and I were in the first stages of discussing how to split household responsibilities, finances, child care, and school and work schedules after we would no longer be married, I got two flat tires in less than two months and my car battery died. This was no coincidence. The message was clear—I was going to wreck myself if I didn't soon check myself and create a healthy way to balance our separation.

I tossed Brian's words around in my mind: "Over the weekend—again?" And I thought back to another time when my work schedule didn't line up with my parenting responsibilities. I was in the final stretch of shooting my TV show, *The Last Goodbye*, when I was asked to fly to Los Angeles for the weekend. If I agreed to travel, it would mean asking Brian to rearrange his days with Jakob and Sam to accommodate me. It seemed like a lot of hassle that I'd rather not do, so I asked for guidance: "Am I supposed to go?"

I instantly got a flash in my mind's eye of a green light, my sign for "go," along with a clear sense of why it would be well worth my time to leave my boys: I clairsentiently felt the spirit of a young boy who had recently died and who was desperate to connect with his mother. My heart ached for them both, and my decision was made. The next day, I packed my bags for the West Coast. Sam pleaded with me to stay home, which didn't make my last-minute packing any easier. I squeezed him and promised him that we would talk on the phone every day I was away and that my job was not more important than him, but that this week another mommy who was missing her son needed my help.

The next day, as I sat down with the mother, Kristin, I instantly sensed her heavy energy; it felt as if it were hanging on me. When I locked eyes with her, it was like we'd switched bodies. I was overcome with a deep sadness and longing. I put my hand up to my heart as if there were a gaping hole I wanted to cover.

"It's okay," I said. "He's here."

Kristin began to tear up.

I sensed again the presence of her son's spirit, and this time he flashed into my mind's eye an image of my oldest son, Jakob, who has a strong and determined personality.

"I'm getting that your son was a big force in life," I said, "and he's also showing me black spots all over his body, which is my sign for cancer."

"That's right," she said as the tears began to fall. "He died of cancer one year ago."

"He knows that his death devastated you, but he's patting you on the back. He's showing me a big, illuminated book, which is my sign for the book of life." I explained to Kristin my understanding that we each have a record book on the Other Side that lists the progress and lessons we learn throughout our lifetime. "He's pointing to your book and saying he's proud of the work you've done on his behalf. Do you know what he's talking about?"

"Yes, I think I do." Kristin explained that after her son died, she set up a foundation in his honor to bring awareness to childhood cancer.

"He's jumping up and down, as if to say 'That's it.' This is your life's work."

Kristin looked at me, confused.

The spirits of children, even babies, often communicate to me that they came into a human body for only a short window of time expressly to help a living loved one learn a powerful lesson or do purposeful life work. I said to Kristin, "It's as if his death created this opportunity for you both to help many more children and serve other parents dealing with a similar loss. He's now acting as your silent partner on the Other Side, leaving you to do all the work here on earth, while he guides you and cheers you on in spirit." I smiled at the image he now flashed in my mind. "He's making a comparison of himself to a personal trainer cheering someone on during an intense workout."

Kristin smiled, too. "I'm obsessed with CrossFit."

"Aha," I laughed. "That's why he's using that reference." I paused for a moment while he downloaded me with more information. "He's also giving me the impression that you're really tired. He's making me feel run-down and sleepy."

Kristin let out a long exhale. "It's been a long year. I feel pretty exhausted."

"'Slow down,' he's saying. He doesn't want your grief and the work you're doing with the foundation to impede your ability to enjoy your life. He wants you to find peace and balance."

Kristin took a deep breath. "Striking that balance is hard, but I will try."

I encouraged Kristin to trust that her son's spirit is always with her. "You're not alone. He hears your thoughts and prayers, so call on him and trust that he will answer."

I thought of my own boys back home in Denver. Even when I'm not physically with them, my spirit is. Our departed loved ones are with us in the same way.

As I DROVE toward my downtown office, I shook the memory of Kristin's reunion with her son and turned up the Shawn Mendes track "A Little Too Much" now playing in the car. How apropos, I thought. Would I be taking on too much if I worked over the weekend? I wouldn't be traveling out of town this time—I'd just be in my Denver office doing readings. Still, I wondered if I was making the right choice: work over family? Maybe my time would be better spent at home with Chris and the kids? Just as I considered this, a car pulled in front of me with a number sequence of 777 on the license plate. One of the most common ways in which our angels, guides, and the departed speak to us is by showing us repetitive number sequences, and I knew immediately what 777 meant: You're on the right track.

"Ha!" I said and took a deep, calming breath, feeling certain that my Team Spirit was with me, validating that my instincts to go to work were right.

But then, not a minute later, I stopped to get gas, and the pump turned off on its own at $43.23. I did a double take. The address of the house Chris and I had recently toured was 4323 Ash Street. Now I was really confused.

Chris and I had recently decided it was time to move into a new house. We needed more room for the seven of us, and also we were living in the same house that Brian and I had lived in for years. We'd made it work so far, but Chris and I both agreed that we wanted a neutral space, a fresh start. A place that was just ours. In recent meditations and in recurring dreams, my guides had shown me real estate signs, and when a pipe burst in our downstairs furnace, flooding the entire basement, I felt sure these were all "signs" pointing toward a move.

But where to? The available listings in Denver were extremely limited, and nothing stayed on the market for long. We were having a hard time finding a home that could accommodate our large family at a price we could afford until we toured 4323 Ash Street. Plus, the moment I spotted the master bedroom with the built-in bed frame, I felt strongly that the house was meant for us.

Let me explain.

For the past year, we've been sleeping on a single mattress on the floor because the old frame was creaky and woke Chris up in the middle of the night. He took it apart one day trying to fix the "squeak," and when he couldn't, we decided to just get rid of it. Since then, we hadn't found a new frame we were all too crazy about. When we started talking about moving, we agreed that we'd wait to buy a new bed frame until after we moved into our new home. Well, now we'd found one with a bed frame already waiting for us.

"I think this might be our house," I said to Chris.

Except, he pointed out, we'd have to come up with a sizable down payment in thirty days if we wanted to compete for it. While my intuitive hit was that this was *our* house, I wasn't sure how to sort out these pesky earthly details.

As I pulled back onto the road, I said, "Guides, I need another sign. Work this weekend, or continue the house hunt? Please give me a clear direction forward." I mumbled under my breath, "And no flat tires, please."

When I got into the office, I noticed that my executive director Jacqui had left a book for me on my desk chair. It caught me off guard. The face of the woman on the jacket cover looked so much like me that I approached it with both curiosity and some suspicion. Once I picked it up, I noticed another resemblance. The woman on the cover sat in the lotus position wearing a sweatshirt with the word "GRATITUDE" across the front. Chris had bought me a nearly identical T-shirt from our favorite yoga studio that I wear as a nightshirt. In fact, it was the shirt I'd woken up in that morning!

Who is this? I didn't recognize the author's name. I opened it to the title page and saw that it was inscribed. "Dear Rebecca, even though you probably don't remember me, I will never forget you. You changed my life forever by starting me on my spiritual path. I wanted to share a copy of my new book with you, which I was guided to write after my reading with you."

I looked at her name again—Ali Katz—and searched my mind for a memory. Ali . . . Ali . . . Ali . . . Aha! I remembered now. I'd given this woman a reading probably five years earlier. It all came flooding back. She'd come to me, seeking guidance about her career path. She was no longer happy at her high-level corporate job, and her mother's spirit came through and pointed her in a different direction. Mom clairvoyantly showed me Ali sitting in the lotus position, just as she now appeared on the cover of her book! I'd told her then that her mom was guiding her to try meditation and yoga. Ali had dismissed the guidance at the time, saying something like "Yoga doesn't pay the bills," but in the five years since the reading, she'd clearly taken her mother's advice to heart.

I flipped to her author bio at the back of the book. Ali described herself as a late bloomer yogini who'd changed her career path at age thirty-five and had finally achieved "balance" in her life. I laughed out loud at this full-circle moment and the clear theme that was emerging. "I get it!" I said out loud for my departed loved ones and guides to hear. "It's all about balance!"

I sat down with a fresh cup of coffee and thumbed through Ali's book, remembering a similar reading I'd had with a woman named Kelly about achieving more work-life balance. Kelly's father, George, who'd died when she was fifteen years old, came through with urgency like he'd been waiting a very long time to speak to her. It had been nearly thirty years since his death, Kelly told me, so indeed he had been waiting awhile. He showed me a white lab coat, my sign for someone who works as a health care provider or doctor.

Kelly confirmed that she'd been a radiologist for years, but quit when her two boys became teenagers. "I wanted to give my sons what I didn't have—a strong parent on their side as they went through the pivotal teenage years."

"Your dad is acknowledging this professional sacrifice you made to stay home with your sons, but he wants you to go back to work," I said. "He's waving his hand forward as if to say 'Keep going.'"

Kelly's father then flashed in my mind a passage from a book I'd read called *Advanced Energy Anatomy* by Dr. Caroline Myss. I'd highlighted a passage where she discusses the difference between work, career, and vocation. To break it down simply, she argues that work is something we do to survive; a career often provides us with higher pay and a professional identity; and our vocation feeds our passion and fulfills our true purpose. I'd been especially intrigued by her definition of vocation and so now I connected the dots.

"I'm getting that Dad wants you to fulfill your true purpose." I paused for a moment while George impressed another image in my mind. "Why is he showing me hospice care?"

She looked at me in absolute shock and explained that her aging mother had gotten sick two weeks prior to our reading and that she'd had to call in hospice. Along with a rotating team of nurses and aides, Kelly had sat at her mother's side, she explained, tending to her in every way she could.

"That's it. Dad is saying, 'to comfort those in need.' This could be through hospice or whatever you choose, but he's clear that you're meant to extend your natural healing gifts beyond your own home."

I shifted in my chair, as Dad impressed me with a feeling of unease and physical tension. The sensation instantly threw me back to a period of time in my own life when I was resisting my true calling and as a result, battling with depression.

"Dad worries that if you continue to stay home, you may become depressed."

Kelly took a deep breath when I said this and admitted, "I wake up every day feeling kind of lost, like my life is off-track and I don't know why."

When clients like Kelly come to me and confess that they feel like something is missing from their life, their loved ones in spirit almost always confirm that they aren't quite yet fulfilling their true purpose. And because of this, their life feels imbalanced.

"Your dad is validating this," I said. "You feel off track because you are." George flashed a mask in my mind's eye and I interpreted it this way. "You're hiding behind your role as a stay-at-home mom. While this is an important part of who you are, on a deeper level you *know* you're meant to be doing more with your time here on earth, and your depression is your sign that you need to make a change, get out of fear and resistance, and follow your intuitive guidance—what your heart is telling you to do."

"But what about my boys?" She dropped her head into her hands. "They need me."

George used my personal frame of reference to help me answer Kelly's concern. He showed me an image of my sons Sam and Jakob doing homework after school and being looked after by their babysitter until I get home. With a full-time working mother, this is their "normal," and they accept it.

"Your boys will be okay. They understand on some level, too, that they have to share you with the world, and that by doing what's right for you, you're doing right by them."

YOU ARE ENOUGH

Like George did for his daughter Kelly, spirits come through often to give their living loved ones an encouraging pat on the back for all they have done, are doing, and are working toward, and also to assure them that they can't do it all. And that's okay. Our daily, hard efforts are enough. This sentiment is a challenging one for most people to accept. We live in a culture, if not a world, of not being or doing enough. We focus on our imperfections and where we believe we fall short.

One of my favorite authors, Brené Brown, has a lot to say about this in her vulnerable and wise book, *The Gifts of Imperfection*, which I've had on my nightstand since it came out in 2010. Brené's message supports what I hear often from the Other Side. Spirits recognize only after they've died that their human quest to get it all done was futile and that the voice that told them they were failing, messing up, or not measuring up was dead wrong. From the Other Side, spirits look at their living loved ones with compassion they didn't afford themselves in life and pass on their heartfelt pleas to stop pursuing perfection. *Give yourself credit for how much you are doing and then give yourself a break*, they say. *Honor your good intentions and all that you do in a day, and leave it at that.*

AFTER THUMBING THROUGH Ali's book for another ten minutes, I closed my eyes to mentally prepare for my first small group reading of the day. After several deep meditative breaths—where I invited in only the presence of loving, supportive, and enlightened beings—I asked out loud, "God, guides, and spirits, what do you want me to know?" When asked, the departed will begin to flash mental movies and short clips of information into my mind's eye that they want me to pass on to their living loved ones. As I should have expected, a balance scale came into clear focus as the pressure changed in the room. I sensed the presence of at least a dozen spirits lining up at the doorstep of my mind, eagerly waiting for me to flip over the OPEN sign.

Showtime.

As I walked into the adjacent reading room and greeted my intimate group of eight, I recognized that they did not appear to know each other, but I understood well that this seemingly random group of strangers was anything but accidental. At some point over the next two hours, they would realize that their departed loved ones had brought them together on this day and at this exact time for a reason. While everyone who attends one of my small groups is guaranteed an individual reading, typically the spirits that show up have banded together ahead of time to deliver parallel insights to the entire group. This is why it's not unusual when people realize that they share similar challenges, situations, and circumstances with everyone in the room. I've led groups where the majority of the attendants lost a loved one to suicide, a child to an incurable disease, or a spouse to betrayal. I've connected groups of grieving widows to their deceased spouses, brothers to brothers, mothers with mothers—and I won't forget the group reading when five out of eight women were similarly wrestling with whether they should leave their marriages. As I looked around this intimate circle, I wondered what parallel message the spirit world wanted me to pass on to the living today.

"For the next two hours," I said to the group, "trust that you are exactly where you need to be. Your departed loved ones and spirit guides have brought us together. Relax in this knowing and trust that you are safe and that if you're open to it, you will receive today exactly what you need."

I continued, "A question I often get asked is: How can I communicate with my departed loved ones? My short answer is presence, by turning down your mind and focusing on the here and now. This isn't always easy to do, but when our minds are quiet, free of endless worry and chatter, spirits have a much easier time being heard, felt, and seen. So take a moment now to turn down your thoughts and let Spirit in."

The room fell quiet and the first spirit to step forward was of an older woman who flashed the word *stroke* in my mind, along with a strong sense of unsettledness and worry. I put the two together. "I'm sensing a spirit who died from a stroke and who was a kind of worrywart in life."

"That sounds like my wife," one of the men in the group held his hand up. "Emily spent her days fretting about getting everything done. I was constantly trying to get her to slow down and enjoy her life more." He paused before continuing, "Well, she didn't slow down, and she eventually had a stroke."

"She's here," I said. "And she's acknowledging that she wasted a lot of time worrying. If she would have known then what she knows now—that the to-do list will never get done—she would have relaxed more."

There was a collective sigh of recognition from the group. I said, "This is something I hear from spirits a lot: However much we do, our minds tend to create more for us to do, and then we beat ourselves up for never seeming to get it all done. We will all die with an unfinished list, and in the end, it doesn't matter!"

SHORTEN YOUR TO-DO LIST

What spirits and my own glimpse at the Other Side have helped me understand is that before each of us is born, we set up very ambitious plans or to-do lists for our lives, and we're not expected to get it all done. Let me say it again: We're not expected to get it all done. I don't know about you, but this sure is a relief to me. In my own life, it can sometimes get to be a little too much. I can become overwhelmed and irritated by the small stuff, like a broken Internet connection or misplacing my car keys. When this happens, I try to pause and consider what I'm giving my energy, care, and attention to, because I know that in the end, it's all small stuff. Do you ever do that—sweat the big and small details? I sometimes draw a mental pie chart of where my energy is going on any given day and on any given hour—to work, kids, the family pet, my marriage, myself. I encourage you to try this. It can be an eye-opening exercise!

On days when I feel especially pulled or overwhelmed, Chris helps me to put it in perspective. He's a man who is constantly juggling, and somehow he's learned better than I have how to let things go and not sweat it. In addition to being an active and involved father to his three girls and my two boys, he's running several companies at once. Yet it seems not to matter how challenged or stretched he is at work or at home, he always puts his heart and humor front and center. It's only at the end of the day after the kids have gone to bed that we'll finally have a chance to sit together alone. This is when Chris will download, and sometimes unload, the demanding moments of his day. A financial setback, an employee dispute—it could be anything, and Chris miraculously rises above the inconvenient earthly details and trusts that a solution will present itself. He'll often shrug and say, "I've done my best, and I've done enough. There's no sense worrying about how it'll all work out because I know that it will, as it should, in just the right time."

Hey, that's my line.

Spirits communicate that the end goal of our lives is not perfection, completion, or scratching everything off our lists; rather, it is about setting our intention and effort to do our best along the way. Focusing on quality over quantity is how we achieve balance. The departed emphasize that the quality of attention and care we pay toward the lessons and plans we set up to learn in our lifetime is what matters most. But instead, most of us focus on quantity—how much we can get done in any given day, week, month, and year. The result is a life that feels like a mad dash, where we rush from one location, promotion, relationship, and milestone moment to the next.

This race, spirits and my guides assure me, is not the pace we should strive for. They will show me a turtle as a sign to "slow down" and have relayed that when we hurry through our days, not only do we struggle and beat ourselves up unnecessarily when we don't accomplish all we set out to do, but our haste causes us to miss what's most important—being present and showing up in loving service to ourselves and to the people in our lives. Spirits are constantly extending their apologies to their partners, children, and friends for not giving them more attention and love when they had the chance. They also express regret for not doing more to nurture and enjoy themselves while they were alive.

Furthermore, when we're constantly on autopilot, going through the motions to do more, get more, and be more, we sometimes miss the bigger lessons we're meant to learn in our lifetime like, paradoxically, surrender, patience, and faith in something bigger than ourselves. When we sidestep these lessons, guess what? They wait for us on the Other Side. In other words, they're still on your to-do list! So we each might as well take our time and be thoughtful, caring, and thorough in whatever we do from moment to moment, and only then move on to the next thing.

How I Use This in My Life: **STRIVING FOR BALANCE**

When your plate feels more than full and you feel weighed down by daily demands, close your eyes, take a few deep breaths, and voice your frustrations and fears. Tell your departed loved

ones and guides what's making you sweat. Then, hand it over—
the big and the small stuff. Envision placing your worries, bur-
dens, expectations, and your to-do list in Spirit's hands.

Let go of your attempt to do it all and trust that your Team
Spirit will support and help you to strike the right balance. Say:
"Help me to balance my life. Fill me with patience and trust
that it will all work out, as it should, in divine timing. Today, I
did my best, and I've done enough."

After relaying the message to the group that our to-do lists will never get
done, I moved on to a spirit who was showing me a red stoplight and a house.
I asked, "Is anyone here thinking of moving or in the midst of moving?"
("Besides me," I thought to myself.)

A woman named Stephanie raised her hand. "I'm in the process of selling
my business and moving out of Denver."

"Who is Joe?" I asked. "A spirit is present who died of lung cancer."

"That's my dad," she asserted.

"Dad's here, and he's clearly saying it's not time."

Stephanie furrowed her brow. "But it's already in motion."

"I'm getting that it's not 'if' but 'when.' He's showing me the month of
May on a calendar. He's also showing me a document that he's signing. Is
there a glitch in the current contract?"

Stephanie looked surprised that I knew this detail, but nodded. "We
haven't been able to finalize the terms."

"Dad is saying something isn't right and to wait. Don't rush it." He continued to flash the month of May in my mind. "Wait and trust that the right
person will come along when the time is right, most likely in the spring."

As I delivered this message to Stephanie, I couldn't help but wonder if
her father's message was also meant for me. His heed to his daughter—don't
get ahead of yourself—felt so relevant to my own moving situation. While I
felt certain in my heart that the house at 4323 Ash Street was meant to be
ours, it wasn't that clear on paper. The financial piece wasn't adding up,
and so I felt like I was wrestling with the Universe, feeling strongly that I

knew the direction our family was meant to go but not sure how we were going to get there.

IN MEDITATIONS AND channeled readings, my guides use a giant watch to communicate how the human mind tends to get ahead of the pace of the Universe. It's like as soon as we think it, we want it to materialize. Poof! But divine timing, spirits have shown me, tends to unfold much more patiently and thoughtfully. As far as Chris and I moving, could it simply be that our eagerness is a step ahead of what the Universe can deliver? Should we also remain confident that it's really just a matter of when, not if?

I resolved to take my own advice when I said to Stephanie, "Dad is saying give it some time. In the meantime, try not to think too much on how or when it's going to happen. Hold tight and know that it *will* happen." In other words, give the Universe a minute to catch up.

CHAPTER 3

RELEASE YOUR SPIRITUAL WEIGHT

After that first amazing group reading of the day, I checked my schedule and realized I had a free hour before my next client. Time for a breather. It's so rare that my days have these breaks. I thought, "Maybe I have time to squeeze in a short yoga class before my next reading?" I craved physical movement. My left hip was throbbing, and I'd been distracted by a feeling of heaviness in my body all morning, and now quite literally I needed to unbutton my pants and breathe.

It started when I pulled on my favorite jeans this morning, only to stop midway. They were so tight I could hardly get them over my hips to cinch the waist. Maybe they'd shrunk in the wash? I tried on another pair. And another. They were *all* tight. My anxiety kicked in. How in the world could I have blown up like this in just a few days' time? I hadn't done anything different, no sudden change to my diet or exercise level. Were my hormone levels off? Maybe my metabolism was slowing down? I'm nearly forty—maybe a gradual bulge is inevitable?

I began to sink into that oh-so-familiar place of self-loathing, where I beat myself up for not maintaining an "ideal" weight. "Ugh," I thought, "I am so *over* feeling this way and spending my limited time and energy obsessing on the number on the scale." Again, my energy is so much better spent when I focus less on the small stuff and more on the real life and death stuff.

I know this, but the truth is, nearly every day I struggle with my body.

There, I said it. I'm embarrassed to admit that I do care about how I look and how my jeans fit. Knowing what I do about what we're really made of and what happens to our bodies after we die, I kick myself for not being above petty weight concerns and the desire to "fit in." Spirits, after all, have been communicating to me for years that we waste too much time on surface-level worries. Our physical body, they've shown me, is simply the temporary vehicle—the rental car, if you will—that we bang around in while we're here and that it's ultimately our soul, our eternal awareness, that endures and continues to expand well beyond our pant size after death.

And even though *I know this*, I'm human just like everyone else, and there are days when I have a tendency to lose sight of what I'm really made of: my insides, not my outsides. I have a body, I *am* a soul.

FAMILY REUNIONS

We're Not Our Outsides

Oliver was a recent widower who came in for a reading to seek closure and comfort after his wife's death. As we sat together, I sensed a strong female presence right away, and I clairvoyantly saw in my mind's eye the movie title *Curly Sue*.

"Who is Sue?" I asked him.

"That's my wife."

I smiled. "She's loud and clear, a big personality."

The departed come through with the same distinct personalities they had in life. Some are shy, serious, and quiet while others are loud, funny, and, on occasion, bossy and hard to deal with. Sue was confident, and I felt her excitement to reconnect with Oliver.

"It's like she's bubbling over with all she wants to tell you," I said. "First she wants to thank you for helping her to cross over, and that everything you said and believed to be true actually *is* true."

Oliver explained that he was a psychologist and had been on his own spiritual path for years, but that his wife Sue had always been a skeptic. "Her belief was that when you die, you die. That's that. When she got sick, I shared my beliefs with her anyway. I sat with her many times, reassuring her that there was a 'heaven' and she was going somewhere beautiful and real. Toward the end, it seemed to give her a sense of peace, but she wasn't entirely sold." Oliver laughed a little.

"Well she's a believer now," I said. "She's showing me that as her physical body was dying, her spirit released and began the journey back home. And as it did, she graduated to a higher level of awareness, like advancing from one school grade level to the next, where she reflected on her life." (Spirits refer to this consistently as one's "life review.") "She's flashing in my mind clothes, expensive jewelry, and looking at herself in the mirror, as if when she reviewed her life, she finally saw how attached she was to material things."

Oliver looked at me in amazement. "That was Sue. She loved her things. She spent a lot of money on cosmetic surgeries and clothes and just a lot of material stuff."

"It's like she's admitting now that she lost herself in life, identifying with and defining herself by her material possessions and her physical appearance. And once she crossed over and the physical world faded away, she felt so much relief to be finally free of all the earthly possessions and pretenses she felt a prisoner to."

I could physically *feel* her relief, and Sue's spirit continued to impress me with an awareness that I've sensed in many readings. Her spirit communicated that, in life, she believed that how she looked on the outside would fill her on the inside, but that as much as she amassed or augmented her appearance, she still felt empty and incomplete. Now in death, she understood that she'd invested her time and energy poorly. She'd short-changed her spirit, where the only true currency is love.

Oliver could hardly believe this was the same woman he'd spent more than 40 years of his life with. He began to cry. "I'm just so relieved and happy that she's found peace. I always wanted this for her."

"She's thanking you again for being her spiritual teacher in life, even though she didn't fully recognize or appreciate your role while she was here. She wasn't the best student, but now she gets it."

"Better late than never," Oliver smiled tenderly.

"And one more thing—she wants you to give away her material belongings. She's showing me jewelry."

Oliver laughed at this. "No way. I don't dare touch it! She has a very expensive and treasured collection of jewelry from around the world. I've purposely held on to it because I know how much it meant to her."

"She's waving her hands as if to say 'let it go.' There's no sense holding on to it. It's only taking up mental and physical space."

"Really?" Oliver said doubtfully.

"She's showing me children, grandchildren maybe, that you could pass it on to, to keep her memory alive. The only thing that matters now is the sentimental value placed on it. Beyond that, it's just stuff. She doesn't need it, and neither do you."

Today, as much as I'd tried to get over my stuff, I was still stuck. My pants were tight, and I felt uncomfortable in my own skin. I resigned that I wouldn't have enough time to go to a yoga class before my next reading, so instead I guzzled down a 24-ounce bottle of lemon water and plopped down on an oversized pillow in my office to pray and meditate. I closed my eyes and set the intention to release the pileup of critical thoughts clogging my mind that were only serving to create more self-loathing and suffering. I repeated like a mantra in my mind, "I have a body, I am a soul. And I am grateful to be alive." I played it over and over like a track in my mind. With every deep breath in and out, I felt myself detach from the heaviness of my physical body and connect with my spiritual body (which doesn't measure on the scale, by the way).

Soon enough I felt the familiar sensation of floating, a feeling of tingly lightness, like I'm expanding out past my physical body and hovering above it. As I floated there, an image of a woman in a wheelchair appeared in the forefront of my mind. I knew immediately who it was: Chelsea, a repeat client of mine.

Five years ago, Chelsea's twenty-year-old son, Sean, died in a tragic motorcycle accident, and the first time I met her she was heavy with grief, as anyone would be after the loss of their only child. Like many parents in this situation do, Chelsea unfairly blamed herself. "There must have been something I could have done to prevent this," she dissolved into sobs at the beginning of the reading. "I should have never let him get that bike." I could feel her choking guilt and all the what-ifs running around in her mind.

Sean's spirit answered the call. His presence came through strong, with a message of reassurance for his mom: He was meant to go when he did. "He's saying that it was technically an accident, but on a soul level, your son knew he was going to leave this world young. If he hadn't died that day in that particular way, it would have been the next day or the day after that."

I asked, "Why is he showing me a pillow, my sign for dreams? Do you dream about him often?"

"I dreamt about the accident a few months before it happened." She was openly weeping now.

"It's not your fault," I cut in. I could clairsentiently feel that she blamed herself for the death, as if she'd somehow manifested it. "Your dream didn't become a self-fulfilling prophecy. Rather, you were subconsciously picking up on what his soul had agreed to do."

Chelsea looked confused.

I explained to her what spirits have communicated to me countless times: We all sign up ahead of time, before we're born, for a particular life experience and we also choose our exit point, or time of death. Spirits refer to this as our "soul contract." I said to Chelsea, "His contract was to go early, and where the motorcycle accident was not planned, it was very much by design."

Sean's spirit showed me that while he was unaware of his soul contract at the time of his death, once he crossed over, he recognized the grand design of it all and understood why he'd been unconsciously tying things up in the days and weeks leading up to his death. He showed me a series of mental pictures that communicated closure—calling old friends, cleaning out his childhood room, and giving away sentimental items to his brother.

"He *had* been doing that," Chelsea gasped. "It was like a compulsion, and I hadn't understood it at the time."

While Chelsea felt some relief and comfort that Sean was now safe on the Other Side, she admitted, "It's still so hard to let him go. I miss him so much." I could feel her heavy heart, a mother's loss and regret. I sensed that she would continue to blame herself for his death and wonder how she could have stopped what Sean's spirit had shown me was inevitable.

Nearly four years had passed when Chelsea came back with her husband, Jason, for a follow-up reading. I hardly recognized my client when Jason pushed her in a wheelchair through my office doors. When Chelsea said hello, her speech was mumbled and nearly incoherent. Jason tenderly explained that his wife had been diagnosed with an aggressive case of ALS, commonly known as Lou Gehrig's disease, which causes muscle weakness and paralysis. I was stunned at her physical transformation since the last time I'd seen her, when she was walking upright and appeared to be perfectly agile and healthy. Now her body was crippled in a chair, and she was writing on an iPad to communicate.

I began the reading by closing my eyes and asking, "God, guides, and spirits, what messages do you have for Chelsea and Jason right now? Thank you for using me as a pure channel to offer them answers and clarity."

As he did four years earlier, Sean's spirit quickly came through, this time with a stronger sense of urgency.

Your son is in the room, and he is clearly saying to you, Chelsea, "It is not your time to die." Using my clairvoyance, Sean showed me the number fifty and a timeline, one of my signs for someone's life span or lifeline.

"Are you fifty?"

"She just turned fifty last week," Jason squeezed her hand.

"Your son is stretching his arms out wide and pointing at a timeline as if to say, "Keep going past fifty. You have many years ahead of you."

Chelsea broke into tears and scribbled words on her iPad. Jason read them: "Part of me just wants to die and be with my son."

"He's shaking his head no, it's not your time to join him."

"Chelsea still blames herself for Sean's death," Jason said, "and thinks she brought the disease on herself."

Chelsea wrote on her iPad and underlined: "I DESERVE this."

Again, I saw Sean closing a set of gates, as if to say that heaven is not yet open to Chelsea. "You've obviously been dealt a game-changing hand with this disease," I said, "but your son is insistent that it's not yet your time to go. His guidance is coming through crystal clear: Don't give up, keep fighting, and you will get through this."

Sean showed me a white lab coat, my sign for doctor, healing and medicine along with an image of my neighbor's son, Tyler, who was diagnosed with muscular dystrophy at a very young age and who has been participating in medical research and testing trial drugs. I put the signs together. "Are you doing tests or involved in some kind of medical trial? I'm actually hearing Sean say 'stem cells.'"

They looked at each other in amazement, and Jason confirmed, "One of the questions we wanted answered today is whether or not Chelsea should pursue treatment—with stem cells! Her doctors have said that it won't cure her of the disease, but could drastically slow down its progression and alleviate many of her debilitating symptoms."

The spirit of Sean started jumping up and down. "Your son is saying, yes, do this! He's showing me the number nine, too. This treatment will extend your life for at least nine more years."

Chelsea looked down at her body and gestured toward her wheelchair, in resignation.

I felt compassion for her, and I leaned in toward her. "You need to forgive yourself and stop thinking you created this disease because you couldn't save your son. It's not your fault. Your son loves you, and it's time for you to love and appreciate the time you still have left in your body." I squeezed her hand and said, "You still have a lot of time left to love your life."

A few days later, Chelsea sent me a touching e-mail. It read: "Thank you. Despite my illness, I now feel inspired to live."

Not only was Chelsea's reading a wake-up call to me then, but it was a slap in the face to me as I sat in my office now. Here I am, a healthy woman worrying over a few extra pounds and pants that don't fit quite right, while Chelsea is struggling day to day with a debilitating disease that has her body confined to a wheelchair. *Shame on me!* Again, I know better than to waste my time on shallow weight stuff. I intuitively knew that my guides had inspired me with Chelsea's memory to remind me of just how fortunate I am to have the use of my body as I do. Over the years, I've been shown a line that circles around the planet multiple times of spirits that desperately want to come into a physical body. The departed recognize that no matter the shape or size, every body is divine and each day is a gift to be in one.

"Forgive me," I said out loud to my guides. "Please free me from this struggle. Change my mind about this. Help me shift my negative, fearful thoughts to love and appreciation of my body."

I continued to repeat this plea for another five minutes, until I felt the judgmental voice in my head begin to lose its power over me. Then, quite miraculously, I felt myself shift into a place of gratitude. (A miracle, after all, is often a simple change in perception.) I thought, "My body is a gift and a blessing. I have a finite amount of time on this planet. I will appreciate my body that allows me to be here." As my appreciation swelled, my tension eased and I really did feel physically lighter all over. I took one final deep breath and thanked God for giving me a healthy body that fully supports me, gets me wherever I want to go, and helps me to carry out my life's work and purpose.

With renewed clarity, I asked my guides if there was anything more they wanted me to know. They flashed in my mind a chocolate chip cookie.

Don't let anybody say that the departed don't have a sense of humor.

While five extra pounds and a bulge around the belly are negligible in the grand scheme of things, my weight gain was real and my guides pointed to what I already knew but was choosing to ignore: *Stop with the emotional eating, already.*

On any given day, I eat pretty healthy. While there's no one size or diet that fits for all, after years of trial and error and trips up and down the scale, I've discovered that for me, eating a high concentration of protein and lots of veggies, along with a daily practice of yoga, walking, meditation, and a good night's sleep, is what serves me the best. Still, I'd be lying if I said I always follow my eating and exercise plan. I'm known to sneak a warm chocolate chip cookie from time to time and then take a nap on the couch.

Sugar has always been my go-to drug of choice when life gets messy. And now that I thought about it, my life had felt a little more disorganized and imbalanced lately, and I'd returned to my old habit of filling up on the sweet stuff to stuff down uncomfortable feelings and worries. I'd been loading up on my half-caff Americanos with artificial vanilla syrup. I'd also been eating well past the point of being hungry, which often meant dessert, and now that I'm being perfectly honest, I'd also been indulging in a glass or two of red wine after work to unwind. While I could blame this behavior on my Jewish upbringing—we use food to comfort, celebrate, and mourn in equal amounts—my eating habits are really my own. Because I'm a medium with deep sensitivity to energy, I will emotionally eat when something's eating me up. I know I'm not alone in this; many of us turn to external sources to feel better.

As I ran through my mental list of recent indulgences, I was reminded of Louise Hay's book *Heal Your Body* where she describes inflammation in the body—often felt as heaviness and physical bloat—as the result of inflamed thinking. It's true that when my weight goes up, it's usually a sign that my mind's running in circles. I realized now that I'd been recently using food to help calm, soothe, and, *okay*, stuff down my fearful thoughts and worries over our impending move, among all the other day-to-day anxieties that inevitably pop up between sunrise and sunset. Rather than ease the discomfort and pain of any emotional situation with a sugary treat, I know that what I should do is put down the fork or the glass and simply go within and ask for guidance.

How I Use This in My Life: **FROM BODY OBSESSION TO FREEDOM**

If you're like me and can get caught up in concerns over food consumption, your body image, or the number on the scale, I encourage you to set a new, healthy intention and ask your guides to help you make the shift from obsessed to free.

Set the intention: Set the intention to release critical thoughts and limiting beliefs about yourself and your body, like "I'll never fit in" or "I'll never lose the weight," and in their place, repeat positive mantras of self-love and acceptance for how you look or eat *today*.

Mentally repeat or say aloud: "My body is a gift and a blessing. Thank you, body, for taking such good care of me and for being the vehicle for my spirit to move around in and carry out my life's work and purpose. I listen to and nurture my body's needs in every moment."

Ask for help: Ask your guides to help you shift thoughts and choices that make you feel bad about yourself. (Setting your intention to think differently is powerful, and you must also *ask for help* to shift your thoughts.) Ask your guides to free you from your body struggle and shift your fearful thoughts. Mentally repeat or say aloud: "Please free me from this struggle. Help me shift any negative, fearful thoughts to love and appreciation of my body Thank you, guides, for helping me to see myself through your eyes. I am perfect as I am, right here, right now."

It's as if once I consciously ask to see things differently, my guides meet me halfway. I notice that my energy will shift just enough to allow me to move through the situation without bingeing on food. Truly, it's that little bit of help from going inward and committing to think, behave, and feel differently that soothes me more than anything I can get my hands on externally.

Signs from the Other Side: **NEGATIVE THOUGHTS CREATE SICKNESS**

In readings with clients, spirits have shown me how negative and worrisome, low vibrational thinking can manifest as inflammation, weight gain, sickness, and even disease. This became clearly evident when I read a woman named Deidre on *The Last Goodbye.* As soon as we sat down together on set, a paternal spirit who identified himself as "Robert" came through with a warning. He clairvoyantly showed me white sugar accompanied by a mental picture of my grandpa who had diabetes. I put the signs together.

"Was your father's name Robert, and did he have diabetes?"

"Yes," Deidre nodded, "and I used to get so mad at him for how he didn't take care of himself."

Robert's spirit raised his hand, as when one swears to tell the truth in court. This is my sign for when a spirit is owning their stuff, truthfully and honestly taking accountability for their actions in life.

"I'm getting a strong sense that he understands now that he made poor choices. He could have lived a healthier life and lived for longer. And now he's shaking his finger at you in a tough love kind of way, as if to throw it back on you. He doesn't want you to follow a similar path. He wants you to learn from his mistakes."

"I could be healthier," she admitted. Deidre was slightly overweight, but not as heavy as her father had carried himself in life, as I clairvoyantly saw. "But I'm so exhausted. I have kids. I work full time, and I just don't care or make it a priority to be 'healthy,' you know?" I could feel her fatigue and depressed thinking, a recipe for self-medicating with food.

"I knew he'd bring this up," she said a little shamefully. "But I'm ready to hear it. I know I should do better."

"He's saying that you can do better. You need to break this family pattern of making unhealthy choices that spiral into low mood swings, and be healthy for your daughter. He's clearly saying this is your destiny."

Deidre's eyes widened, and she looked at me in disbelief. "I can't believe you just said that. That's my daughter's name—Destiny."

When we engage in negative, critical self-talk, we set more negativity into motion. The end result, in many cases, is an unhealthy or even diseased body. This was Robert's warning to his daughter. I passed on a similar message to another young woman named Claire who came in for a reading with her mother. As I opened myself up to messages from the spirit world, I sensed a young male—around fifteen years old—who had recently died. I clairvoy-antly saw him place a hand over his chest, indicating a heart or lung issue. When I mentally asked for more clarity, I clairsentiently felt it was his heart. I asked Claire if she knew anyone like this, and she looked at me wide-eyed. "That's my best friend Phillip. He died four months ago from a heart attack. He'd just turned fifteen."

I felt Phillip's spirit shrinking down as I received a clairvoyant mental picture of a crab in its shell, my sign for being withdrawn or hiding from the world. "I'm sensing that he was a loner in life, too."

Claire nodded. "He was."

"But *you* were his friend."

"Best friend," Claire's eyes welled up with tears.

"He's giving me this feeling like he was really closed off. He's putting his hands over his heart again, as if to say it was closed."

Claire said, "He didn't trust or have a lot of faith in people."

"That's right. His disconnection from other people is what ultimately caused his heart condition and his untimely death. He's showing me on a timeline that he died too young. He wasn't supposed to go that early, and he now understands that one of his big life lessons was to learn how to open his heart to other people—to give and receive love. But instead, he spent most of his life with a hardened heart, and it eventually gave out."

I checked in with Claire to be sure she was following. "Is this all making sense? Once a spirit reaches the Other Side, they come to understand the 'lessons' they were meant to learn while they were alive in a body."

She nodded her head. "Okay, that makes sense."

I continued, "But since he failed to learn his own lesson, now his work on the Other Side is to help the living do what he didn't do." I paused as I received another insight from Phillip. "He's pointing his finger at you, as if to say you must open *your* heart."

I suddenly felt a strong sense of hopelessness and indifference along with a mental picture of Robin Williams, one of my signs for suicide. I asked as gently as I could, "Are you or have you been thinking about suicide?"

Claire's mom drew in a breath. "That's why we're here," she blurted out and began to cry. "Ever since Phillip's death, she's been so down, and since depression runs in our family, I've been very worried."

I said to Claire's mother, "I'm sensing that Claire's depression is not a mental imbalance but a situational mood swing brought on by sadness and grief—but that you should definitely consult with a doctor to be sure and to discuss treatment options."

I shifted my attention back to Claire. "You lost your best friend. It makes perfect sense that you're feeling very sad and low, but your friend wants you to know that you have a long life ahead of you. He's stretching his arms out wide. He's also showing me a drum, as if to say he marched to his own beat. But you can do it differently. You can choose to open your heart and be happy."

Claire finally smiled when she heard this. "He played the drum in the school band. It was one of the few things he loved to do."

NEARLY EVERY DAY, spirits remind me how powerful our thoughts are. As much as our eating habits, our thoughts have the power to weigh us down and manifest as physical discomfort, sickness, and disease. Dr. Masaru Emoto, a researcher and alternative healer from Japan, demonstrated in a dramatic experiment that human thoughts and intentions can alter physical reality. Dr. Emoto placed portions of cooked rice into two containers. On one container he wrote "Thank you, I love you" and on the other "You fool, I hate you." He then instructed schoolchildren to say the labels on the jars out loud every day when they passed them by. After 30 days, the rice in the container with positive thoughts had barely changed, while the other was moldy and rotten.

What's the lesson here? What you eat matters, but so does your attitude toward what you eat and toward your life in general. If I sit down to a plateful of healthy broccoli, but with every bite I curse myself for eating it, what I'm ingesting is really the rotten self-criticism and judgment more than the limited calories from the broccoli itself. As spirits have shown me, negativity isn't easily digestible; it has a way of sticking to your insides, and when you consume it day after day, don't be surprised if those negative stored cells turn into fat or, worse, sickness and disease.

I RETURNED TO my next reading feeling so much clearer. My meditation had really shifted my energy and my mood, and I anticipated that my connection to the Other Side would be that much stronger now. My readings are the clearest when *I'm* clear. When I'm preoccupied or stuck in a negative headspace, I can't connect to my spiritual space. Nor can I really be one hundred percent present for the needs of my clients. My readings are also more accurate when my body is free of artificial ingredients and mood-altering substances like alcohol, sugar, and caffeine. (I've never tried to do a reading with a hangover, but I can guarantee it would be foggy at best.) In the absence of feeling weighed down by inflamed thoughts, emotional eating, or unhealthy substances, I feel clean and light. And it's when I'm in a lightened and heightened state of mind that I can best connect with the higher vibration of the spirit world. This isn't just true for me, but for you, too.

How I Use This in My Life: **MAKING THE SHIFT FROM HEAVY TO LIGHT**

I am hypervigilant about checking in daily, if not hourly, with how I feel mentally and physically because my mediumship abilities, and my livelihood, depend on it. The lighter I feel, the stronger and more sustainable the connection I can make between the two worlds. This is true for everyone really. To better connect to and communicate with the spirit world, you must first clean and clear your body and calm your mind.

When you care for yourself by getting enough sleep, eating healthy, regularly exercising, *and* freeing yourself of negative, weighty thoughts, you will experience an energetic shift from heavy to light. With more buoyant energy, you will likely discover that you enjoy your life more, and you also will be better able to connect to your support system on the Other Side. Every day, I take a mind-body-spirit approach to get in a "lightened" state of mind. Try it for yourself.

Mind: Over time, inflamed thoughts and internalized feelings will build up and weigh you down. Depression, resentments, irritability, and stress are all mood indicators that your mind needs a cleanse. Make it a regular practice to release the internal gunk through journaling or talking it out in therapy or with a trusted support system or friend. Also keep in mind that what we think about most has a way of manifesting in our day-to-day lives. So think healthy thoughts by repeating them as daily affirmations. Replace your negative commentary with the affirmative: "I am healthy and well. I am good enough right now, just as I am."

Body: Give yourself a running start to feeling good physically. Food is one of the most efficient drug-delivery systems we have, and processed foods, caffeine, and sugars really do affect how we feel physically, emotionally, and even spiritually. Help your body and mind clear away the cobwebs by doing your best to eliminate, or significantly reduce, your consumption of artificial ingredients, sugar, caffeine, alcohol, and foods that create inflammation and poor digestion. In addition, try to add some daily movement into your life. It's important to remember that our bodies act like sponges that absorb all energy, both light and dense, positive and negative. When our bodies absorb too much of the heavy stuff, we feel weighed down, irritable, and less and less spiritually connected. If you're soaking up too much heavy energy, you need to find time to wring out your body. Throw down a yoga mat, go on a walk, or take a rigorous Spin class to energetically untangle and release.

Spirit: If you can, make time every day to tend to your spiritual cleanliness. Five minutes of prayer or meditation (sitting or walking) may not seem like much, but it is a highly efficient practice for releasing negative and heavy thoughts. Set the intention to make the shift from heavy to light and ask your guides to help you. When you make a decision, or set an intention, to change or to see things differently, your guides meet you halfway—which oftentimes can be all you need to make a better decision for yourself. And a good decision today leads to another good decision tomorrow.

My next two readings were over the phone. The first was with a client named Bethany. When she answered, I could sense, and literally *feel*, the agitation in her voice. I mentally asked her guides and departed loved ones with her today to send her love, clarity, and ease as this is what I imagined she might need.

"Let's begin," I said. "I believe your mom is with us. I sense a maternal presence to the left of you. Is your mom still alive?"

"She died earlier this year."

"She's here with you now. She's blowing you kisses, thanking you for all that you did for her toward the end. Are you the oldest daughter?"

"Yes," Bethany said, her agitation calming somewhat. "I was the one sibling who was there with her. She died at home with the aid of hospice."

"She's showing me an image of you at her bedside and a feeling of you being totally present with her, holding her in a space of love."

I could hear Bethany begin to cry, as she tried to suppress it.

I continued gently, "She's making me feel like she was really hard on you in life."

Bethany confirmed this to be true. She said she always felt that her mom was the hardest on her and that she was never quite good enough in her estimation.

"Now she's showing me a mattress. I'm not sure where she's going with us, but I'll ask—did you just buy a new mattress or are thinking about buying a new mattress?"

Bethany laughed nervously. "Yes. Just *this* week I went to see my chiropractor and she recommended I buy a new one."

"That's it," I said, understanding the sign and the symbolism. "Your mother dumped on you when she was alive, and you've been carrying the weight of

Mom's judgment your whole life, to the point where you physically have developed back pain. It's as if you've been unconsciously crying, 'Get off my back!'"

Bethany let out a deep sigh of resignation, indicating that the message I was passing on was true. "Mom's sorry for projecting her own stuff onto you. She loves you. She accepts you. And she wants you to be free of that old judgment."

This simple message of acceptance was what broke Bethany open. She cried outwardly now, and I could feel her energy lift and soften.

"I've waited my whole life to hear that."

PARALLEL MESSAGES TEND to come in twos and threes, so I wasn't surprised when my next call with a man named Paul took the same direction as Bethany's.

"I'm sensing a male spirit like a brother. Do you have a brother?"

"I did. He died about ten years ago."

"The spirit is pointing at you and a mother figure in a house. Do you still live at home?"

Paul said, "After my brother Collin died, I moved in with Mom to look after her."

"Well, your brother is saying it's time to move out. He's literally showing me real estate signs and giving me the sense that your mother is a burden to you and that you are enabling her."

Paul sighed, "She has a lot of debt. She's a compulsive online shopper, and I can't get her to stop."

"Your brother is warning that if you don't stand up for yourself and give yourself some relief around this relationship, it will take a toll on your health physically. And it may go cellular."

"I think it already has," Paul admitted. "I tweaked my neck working out, and it won't get better. I've even been to the doctor, and they can't figure it out. It's been months now, and the strain is still there. I haven't been able to go back to the gym, and honestly it's making me kind of crazy."

"Your mother is a pain in your neck," I said, bringing it full circle. "How old are you? Your brother is showing me the number forty-seven."

"I turn forty-seven next month."

"He's saying you have given up too much of your life tending to your mom, and he's urging you to say 'enough' and take care of yourself without feeling guilty. When you're able to do that, your neck pain will likely begin to ease and feel better."

IN MANY READINGS like Paul's and Bethany's, spirits show me how, in addition to our own thoughts and heavy emotions, the energy of the people in our lives can contribute to feeling weighed down. I am especially susceptible to this because I'm an empathetic sponge, and my very work means opening myself up to the energy of the living and the dead. When I don't take steps to set energetic boundaries before readings and also uncover and release the energy I've taken on afterward (I will show you how to do this in just a moment), my physical body can be taken for a ride.

Two nights before I was scheduled to film the final episode of *The Last Goodbye*, I was startled awake with a tap on my shoulder. I opened my eyes. No one was in my hotel room with me—or rather, no physical being was in the room. This form of physical contact from the spiritual realm has only happened to me one other time in my life, but I recognized immediately that a spirit had literally reached out from beyond the shadows and physically touched me. As I lay in bed, I mentally asked who was there. I didn't get an answer, but I intuitively felt that the spirit in the room would visit me on set in the presence of its living loved one.

Later that morning, I started to feel nauseous, but dismissed it as travel fatigue or a lingering winter flu that had swept through our household the month before. As the day turned into evening, however, I began feeling really bad, and maybe this is TMI but the toilet became my constant companion for the next several hours. I wondered what had made me so sick. It was as if my body was undergoing a complete extermination, and I wondered if it was more than just a physical purge—maybe a spiritual release of some sort. As I laid my head on the bathroom floor, I prayed I would recover before filming my final episode of the show. I clairaudiently heard a voice that told me to let the experience pass through me, and I'd be well and fine to arrive on set.

The next morning, just as I'd been "told," I woke up feeling back to my old self. On the drive out to the home where I was to do the filmed reading, my guidance confirmed that I was exactly where I should be: I passed a license plate on the freeway with the number sequence 444, which means your angels and guides are with you, followed by another plate with the sequence 999, which means you're showing up to do God's work. All was well until I arrived on set, and I was again hit with waves of nausea and a heavy emotional feeling of dread, like I was walking into a very dark situation. When I sat down with twenty-one-year-old Livia, I was finally able get a clear read on what I was experiencing physically.

The spirit of a maternal figure pushed forward into my awareness, repeating the words "Beverly Hills" and showing me an image of Rodeo Drive. I asked Livia if that meant anything to her, and she said, "Well, my mom's name was Beverly!"

This was the validation I needed to confirm that Livia's mom was in the room. Beverly's spirit then hit me with an intense feeling of stomach upset. Had this spirit, I wondered, been behind my 24-hour flu? I asked Livia if her mother had been very sick before she died.

"She's making me feel like I've been poisoned."

Tears streamed down her face, as Livia confirmed that her mother had been overmedicated.

"This is kind of graphic," I said, "but was there a lot of vomiting tied to her death?"

"It was everywhere around her body," Livia choked.

That's it. I'd become similarly sick, a form of sympathetic pain where I, the medium, take on the spirit's energy and emotional experience. While a physical reaction this extreme is rare, picking up on the energy and emotions of other beings—the living and the dead—happens to many of us every day, and when you're covered with heavy energy from those around you for prolonged periods of time, your physical and emotional health will inevitably suffer.

How I Use This in My Life: **GET ENERGETICALLY DRESSED**

Mentally surrounding yourself with protective white light works to create an energetic boundary between you and any outside energies, the living and the dead. This practice helps to protect your good mood, thoughts, and feelings throughout the day. I begin this practice by taking a few slow, meditative breaths and then focusing on drawing white light down into the crown chakra, the middle space just above the eyes. Imagine this light flooding in, through, and around your body as you say: "I am connected, protected, guided, and directed."

Getting energetically dressed is as important as remembering to put on fresh underwear in the morning (which is why I often do this practice before I get physically dressed for the day). If you do not protect your energetic body, almost as soon as you begin to interact with the world around you, you are at risk of soaking up the energy of everyone you bump into. Absorbing other people's highs and lows happens all the time. By getting energetically dressed and setting a pure intention, you in effect create a protective boundary between your energy and those around you.

In addition to getting spiritually dressed, I like to take a few minutes before and after every reading I do to clear the room. After my call with Bethany and Paul, I said a short prayer to release the spirits that had helped me deliver messages from the Other Side: "Spirits and the living, I give your energy back to you. I ask that all of my own energy come back into me now, fully and completely." I closed my eyes and mentally drew a big bubble of white light around my body and tapped my feet on the ground, a symbolic act of grounding back into the real world.

As I opened my eyes, I heard a knock on my office door.

"Come in."

"Hi, babe." It was Chris. Did I mention we share office space? It's the perfect yin-yang balance. He consults the living, while I consult the dead.

"Wanna grab lunch later?"

"I have a tight schedule today," I frowned. "How about a late afternoon coffee run?" I made a mental note, *without the artificial sweetener.*

"Sounds good," he smiled and lingered at the door. "You're beautiful, by the way. Inside and out." He winked and shut the door.

I smiled and thanked my guides for inspiring him to tell me exactly what I needed to hear. Like I said, our guides step in when we need them to remind us of what we've already figured out on our own, but from time to time need to be reminded of.

I have a body, I am a soul, and I am grateful for this life.

CHAPTER 4

ABUNDANCE IN ALL THINGS

'd passed on lunch with Chris, but I was still hungry and in need of something. Since I already had to run out to the pharmacy before my afternoon readings, I made a quick stop at the house to make myself a Vega One protein and greens shake. When I don't have time to sit down to a proper lunch, this is my go-to meal in a glass.

I poured my shake into my travel tumbler, and as I turned to pick up my car keys from the counter, I knocked it over. "Not again!" I fumed out loud. This was the second spill of the day. This morning, as I was getting out of the shower, I heard Jakob call from his bedroom, "Mooooom, I need you!" I rushed down the hall in a bathrobe and with wet, tangled hair to discover Jakob's breakfast shake spilled all over his computer laptop and dripping onto the floor. I shrieked out loud, which brought Chris to the rescue. Thankfully, he was able to help me clean it up before it ruined the keyboard, but still, the accident added more craziness to what tend to be already frazzled mornings.

And now I'd spilled *my* shake and I didn't have time to make another one before returning to the office. I began to hastily wipe it up off the counter when I noticed it had spread underneath a stack of receipts. I picked up the drippy stack, and for no good reason really, I scanned through the Costco receipt on the top, from a trip I'd recently asked our babysitter, Kat, to make to pick up a few things. As I did, my stomach tightened with a sense of unease. Something wasn't adding up. There on the receipt were a number of items like bath towels and bedding that I didn't remember asking her to buy.

Come to think of it, I didn't recall seeing any of these things around the house either. Then I saw that several gift cards were included in the total, and that's when I was suddenly struck with clairvoyant guidance. In my mind's eye, I saw a dagger sticking me in the back. *Ouch!* Intense and scary, yes, and I knew exactly what it meant. I'd been lied to.

In the car on the way back to the office, I fought with what I knew to be true and what I wanted to believe. For the past few months, I'd had my suspicions that Kat wasn't always being honest with us. A mom—even a busy working mom—can sense when something is amiss at home, even if she's too frazzled to investigate what it is in the moment. I'd noticed subtle things, like her avoiding eye contact and giving vague answers, and I'd even had a dream in which Kat was wearing different Halloween masks, a clear sign that she was hiding something in real life. But I chose to ignore what felt to be little, insignificant untruths because I really didn't want my suspicions confirmed. Kat had been caring for my boys for over five years, and now she was looking after Chris's girls, too. Our kids loved her, and I considered her like a little sister to me. In other words, she was like family. But as I drove back toward the office, I had the unmistakable claircognizance, the clear knowing that I'd been violated by someone I had trusted.

THE HEAD-HEART CONFLICT

Clients often ask me, how do you know if your "hunch" is right and not a projection based on fear or a conclusion based on other people's opinions? We all get intuitive hits like the one I'm describing, but we often second-guess our knowing. Our minds take over, and we overthink and overanalyze to the point that we dismiss our feelings because we can't prove them in the moment. But what I've learned over the many years of doing mediumship work, where I must rely on and trust my intuition to connect with the unseen world, is that even if your hunch isn't validated right away, nine times out of ten it's proven true over time. In my life, my initial read on a situation is likely to be right. This is why I'm always telling my clients: Believe in what you feel.

So often we try to make sense of things from a mind level versus honoring, listening to, and trusting the wisdom and guidance that rises up from deep within. Your feelings, not your thoughts, are your best guidance because your feelings are the language of your Higher Self, that wise inner voice that says I-know-what-I-know. Whenever I feel overwhelmed by a feeling—either physically or emotionally—I know it's my Higher Self whispering in my ear (or sometimes hitting me over the head), *Acknowledge what you know to be true.* While it can be easy to dismiss feelings, what we intuitively feel points us toward the truth, without fail. And the key is to listen to and act on this guidance before your mind interferes.

Now, having found that Costco receipt, I wrestled with what I had to do: Confront Kat and likely let her go. I was overwhelmed by what this would mean. Our kids would have to say good-bye to a caregiver they loved, and Chris and I would have to search for another babysitter, one we could trust. I shook my head with hurt and disappointment, not only because I knew I'd been betrayed by someone who was like family, but also that I'd found myself in another situation where someone was taking advantage of me—this time by stealing from within my home.

"Why does this keep happening?" I said out loud in the car, and the words caught in my throat. Of course, I knew the answer. Kat had taken advantage of me because I'd enabled her to do so. I'd entrusted her to manage the kids' social calendar, shop for the family, and even pay some of our household bills, and when she let things slip here and there, I looked the other way and didn't say a word. For months I'd been making mental excuses for her because I'd somehow convinced myself that I was the caregiver in the relationship. It was my responsibility, I'd told myself, to provide her with a steady job and a dependable paycheck, whatever the cost to me.

I realized now that this had been a big mistake, because by doing this, I'd given my power away. "It's that life lesson again," I thought to myself—learning to distinguish the fine line between helping someone and hurting myself. I've always been a people-pleaser, a giver and caretaker by nature. My guides continue to remind me that there's nothing spiritual or healthy about staying quiet and denying my own needs to serve another. I've paid the price of not getting this lesson right too many times. And really, how many times does the Universe need to test me before I wake up and recognize the patterns I keep repeating? Life tests each of us in different ways, urging and pushing us to learn our most important lessons until we get them right, and even with my access to Other Side insight, I can be the slowest of learners.

I thought about the situation with Kat and how often my powerlessness translates into a financial loss. I guessed this made sense since money—what we earn, how much we have or do not—is simply a paper exchange for our worth. Sure, we each earn money in exchange for what we "do," be that our talent, time, or service, but what spirits communicate is that what we earn is more directly based on the value we place on our *worth*. Once they reach the Other Side, many spirits enter what looks like a restorative day spa where they heal their sense of self-worth by recognizing we are all deserving in God's eyes.

FAMILY REUNIONS

Measuring Your Worth

"I'm sensing a father figure. Is your dad still alive?"

"He died two months ago," my client Lilliana said.

"He's here with you now, and he wants me to talk about you packing. Are you packing to go somewhere?"

Lilliana laughed and said she almost didn't make it to the reading because she was literally moving out of her house and into her boyfriend's home this afternoon.

"I was going to cancel the reading, but instead I just left the movers alone at my house for an hour because I felt so strongly that I needed to hear whatever messages you might have for me."

"Dad is saying that you should not go through with the move." I regretted delivering this news as I didn't want to upset Lilliana. I mean, movers were at her house right now! But her father had an urgency to his message.

I said, "Your dad is holding up a firm hand in protest. He's telling me that he doesn't think you should go through with it."

Lilliana slunk back into her chair.

"Remember that no matter what Dad is telling you, you still have free will. Meaning, you can do whatever you want. It's your life."

Lilliana dropped her head and began to cry, and as she did her father's spirit continued to flash mental pictures of dollar bills along with a strong feeling of physical pressure and stress on my shoulders. I felt fairly certain I knew what Lilliana's dad was trying to say: She felt unhappy in the relationship and deserved an equal who valued her for who she was.

When Lilliana finally looked up, she said, "Everything about my boyfriend is perfect on paper, but he's not right for me. I've known this for a long time."

As Lilliana and I continued to sit together, she explained that she'd been told from a young age by both of her parents that she wasn't "the smartest apple in the bunch" but that she'd always be pretty. "My dad basically told me to use my looks to get what I want in life."

As a result, Lilliana had spent her entire life emphasizing her beauty as her only currency of worth. She admitted that she'd relied on every man in her life, as she was doing now, to financially support her because she didn't believe she could support herself.

"Dad is saying he is sorry," I said. "He's extending an olive branch and asking for your forgiveness. Part of his work now on the Other Side is to help you change your mind about this and finally find someone who values all of you, the inside and out, and who you truly love in return. He's showing me coins are his sign to you."

Lilliana gasped and pulled a coin out of her purse. "Dad used to collect rare coins. As I was boxing things up this morning, I found this one. I have no idea where it came from."

"It came from your dad in heaven," I said. "He wants you to believe in your true worth. He sees it now and he wants more than anything for you to value *yourself*."

When spirits speak about worth, they're hardly ever talking about money and "net" worth but about self-worth. I've done countless readings where spirits regret how they focused so much on their material status in life, and it wasn't until they died that they realized you don't take anything material with you! In my mind's eye, spirits rip up documents and throw money up in the air, indicating that their worth on paper no longer matters on the Other Side.

I've connected with countless spirits who pass on the following message to their loved ones: When you advocate for what you need and deserve and increase the value you put on *yourself,* you step into your power. What do I mean by power? Certainly not the kind that is misused to control, dominate, or hurt others, but the sense of power that comes from believing in and standing up for yourself. Spirits pass on that it is our birthright to exercise our power, and when we don't—when we feel powerless—we tend to act in ways that cause us suffering. Addiction to food, shopping, technology, drugs, entertainment, sex, excessive physical exercise, and overworking are all signs that you are disconnected from your power. Essentially, you're turning to an external source to temporarily fill you and make you feel more powerful. Financial scarcity and challenges, or a strong desire to amass and maintain material wealth and personal possessions, often indicates a need to feel more worthy, and deserving. If you continue to be confronted by the same difficulties and challenges, whether it's with a person or a situation, this may be a sign that you're sacrificing, settling, or accepting less than you're worth. And finally, the departed repeatedly point to health issues as a physical sign that their living loved one is feeling emotionally powerless. Old anger, resentment, blame, shame, and guilt are powerless emotions that can manifest as physical illness, pain, depression, or disease.

How I Use This in My Life: MAKE THE SHIFT FROM LESS THAN TO WORTH MORE

Spirits visit me in readings and in my personal meditations regularly with a simple and very direct message for the living: Shift your thoughts, actions, and reactions from feeling less to feeling more. So the next time a "spilled milkshake" incident comes up for you, I strongly recommend you take a minute to sit with the experience and inquire within. Ask yourself:

What is this spill trying to teach me? Does this have anything to do with my own sense of worth or how I value myself? Am I playing small? Am I giving my power away? If the answer is yes, then make the shift from "less than" to "worth more" with my mind, body, and spirit approach.

Mind: Ask yourself, "Is there something scary about feeling powerful?" Ask your younger self, "Who told me or made me feel that I wasn't powerful, valuable, deserving, or worthy? Who told me that my needs should always come second?" Journal your thoughts and feelings as they surface, without judging or censoring them. Follow with an affirmation(s) either written or spoken out loud several times: "I am innately powerful. It is my birthright and it is safe for me to be powerful."

Body: What makes you feel strong, vibrant, and physically powerful? Whatever it is, do it more often. For me, it's yoga class, walks in nature, and a clean, healthy diet.

Spirit: If I'm feeling a sense of powerlessness, I will sit in meditation and ask my guides to empower and protect me. I imagine them dressing me as a spiritual warrior by placing a crown on my head, symbolizing my own sense of worthiness; draping a cape over my shoulders and back, symbolizing their protection of me; and placing a sword in one hand, to help me battle powerlessness and fear, and a rose in the other, to remind me to serve the world with love.

When we let others dictate our value and worth, we give away our power. When we let others take advantage of us because we don't put a high enough value on our personal worth, we give away our power. When we put a higher worth on someone else's value than on our own, we give away our power. I had done some combination of all three by looking the other way when I intuitively knew that Kat was being dishonest with me.

Feeling a bit deflated by this realization, I pulled back into my office garage and before cutting the engine, I closed my eyes and asked for help. "Departed loved ones and guides: Help me resolve this situation with Kat. Help me to step back into my power." As I repeated the words, I began to feel the subtle presence of my guides close in around me. *Trust that everything will be all right,* I heard them say. And right on cue, Bob Marley's "Three Little Birds" started to play on the radio. I choked back tears. When my dad was alive, he used to borrow from this song when I needed a boost. "Cheer up, honey," he'd sing to me, "everything's gonna be all right." I opened my eyes and noticed the time on the clock—12:14—my dad's birthday. Both of these signs confirmed that my guidance was real, and with this knowing I felt a sense of calm descend over me, along with the courage to stand up for myself and confront Kat for stealing.

I opened the car door and laughed through tears when I noticed a single dollar bill lying on the asphalt. I took this as a third sign, calling to mind that money will flow back to me when I stop acting as an enabler. When insight or signs come in threes, pay attention! I felt certain that my dad and my guides had put all three together to assure me that everything will be all right, and also to remind me that our thoughts and words are not a one-sided conversation. Spirits listen in and hear our calls for help.

I thought about what I tell clients all the time: We each have a responsibility to recognize the signs sent to us by our guides and then to honor the guidance we get. My guidance was telling me, Rebecca, when you feel worthy and deserving of being treated with respect, kindness, honesty, and love, people will gravitate toward you who want to give you respect, kindness, honesty, and love. As you find the courage and strength to stand up for yourself, you will step back into your power and receive true abundance.

ACCEPT THE RICHES OF THIS LIFE

While spirits have communicated to me that an abundant life isn't really about money or having material things, this isn't to say that we shouldn't enjoy a few riches along the way. When my dad was alive, he loved giving me a hard time about my Lexus SUV. "If you're so 'spiritual,' why do you need a big, expensive, and materialistic car?" he'd tease.

"Because I like to drive it," I'd shoot back.

Spirits communicate that as long as we don't define ourselves by our net worth and our material things, or put more value on them than on our close relationships, our work, service, and purpose, then there's no harm done. Part of the fun of being human, after all, is enjoying the richness of the physical world. Spirits make the point that it is the feeling that a material item or a physical experience gives you that you're really after anyway. A pedicure may help you to feel pampered and cared for (as it does for me). An indulgent meal out may comfort you. A new sports car or an exotic vacation might invoke excitement and daring. The material object is simply the vehicle for a desired feeling. I wasn't attached to my Lexus as a status symbol nor did I define myself by its dollar value. I simply enjoyed driving it, and it made carpooling kids back and forth from school and weekend sports activities with stuffed backpacks and duffel bags much easier. To me, that feeling is worth a lot.

I love recounting the story of Nancy Lee, who was encouraged by her deceased father to take an African safari trip, because it perfectly illustrates this point. During our time together, the spirit of Nancy's father mentally drew a picture in my mind of an African safari. When I relayed this vision to Nancy, she gasped and said she and her sister had been recently researching a trip of this kind but realized the expense was way beyond their budget.

"Your dad is waving his hand forward, as if to say that you should go. He's making me feel that this trip is about more than the money." I explained to Nancy that spirits often encourage their loved ones to focus on the value of an experience rather than its financial cost.

"Easy for him to say," she laughed.

"He's signing a restaurant check," I said, "like he's picking up the bill."

While Nancy enjoyed the idea of her dad paying her and her sister's fare to Africa, she wasn't too sure how a handout from the Other Side really worked. I gave her my usual advice: Trust, have faith in the unknown, and wait and see. When she sent me an e-mail not one week later, she validated how Spirit has a way of creating abundance when we feel worthy of receiving it, even when it doesn't add up logically.

> Rebecca,
>
> I wanted to tell you that during my reading, you told me that I would go on a big trip that was extravagant and asked me if I was worried about the expense. I said yes—the trip cost $31,000! You said my dad really wanted my sister and I to go on this trip. You said it would be a "soul expansion" for us, and you said that Dad would provide the money. That was on a Wednesday morning. Thursday evening I got a call from a woman representing my home insurance company. She said she'd been reviewing my files and noticed that I had been paying for two earthquake insurance policies. This was an oversight that the company should have noticed and she agreed to pay me back what I'd overpaid—$31,000! How about that?

Yeah. How about that?

OVER THE COURSE of looking for a new home for our blended family, there have been times when I've had to stop and really question myself. Why do I want this? Do I really need a bigger house? Because the truth is, Chris and I have all the material comforts we need, and for that I feel blessed. So what is wanting another home all about? What rises to the surface is the *feeling* that a new home will provide me. It's a symbolic new beginning, and with that comes a feeling of relief and excitement for the future. After all, the house we live in now is the house Brian and I lived in for eight of the eleven years we were married. It's within these walls that we also finally decided to divorce. So while it's still a beautiful and spacious home, Chris and I both desire the feeling that fresh walls and a new shared space will give our blended family. This feeling is what I want to buy, and I put a high value on it.

In his estimation, one of the best gifts Chris ever received was during the real estate crash in 2008 when he lost everything and had to file for bankruptcy. Of course, at the time it didn't feel like much of a gift. He was devastated and terrified, but he said the experience made him reevaluate his definition of success, true value, and wealth. Where he once measured his life in dollars and derived his fulfillment from the things his money could buy, after the experience of losing it *all*, he realized that for him, success is measured in joy. I swooned the first time he said this to me because not only is it such a beautiful lens to look through at the world, but also spirits have been communicating to me the same message for years. They add to it—success and wealth is measured in joy, self-worth, and in *love*, the kind you give and receive.

TO RECEIVE MORE, GIVE MORE

In addition to believing you are worthy and deserving to live a life of abundance, spirits encourage the living to give more to receive more. Now, I'm not talking about behaving in a self-sacrificing sort of way (like I have a tendency to do) but to have a general, day-to-day attitude of generosity. This can look like a smile, a kind word, or listening and being present for someone else. Spirits communicate that we do our best work when we show up in loving service.

Chris and I recently experienced how this type of "work" has a magical effect. On a recent run to Target, we got behind a man in the checkout line who came up short of his total bill. We watched him select a few items to put back when Chris quietly pulled a twenty dollar bill out of his wallet and offered it to the cashier. The man turned toward us with a look of confusion, followed by embarrassment, and then insisted Chris put his money away. Chris said, "Please, it's on me. Next time, it's on you."

After another moment of hesitation, he agreed to accept the gesture. As the man thanked us and gathered his items to leave, the cashier handed Chris back a few dollars.

"Your change," she said. "You handed me a twenty, but he was only short $14.40."

Chris and I exchanged a knowing look. Chris's birthday is December 12, so a few years ago he combined the numbers 12 × 12 = 144 to create his own numeric sign for his guides to use when they want to get his attention and make their presence known. (Everyone can do this, by the way. In fact, your guides and departed loved ones appreciate being given a designated sign to use. It makes communication easier!)

"I think my guides were behind this whole exchange!" Chris said in awe. "I was guided to give to this man."

"Or," I said, "they're giving you their nod of approval. Either way, it's a sign to validate what you did. You showed up in service to someone in need. At the end of the day, that's what our 'work' is all about."

Much of the time, our daily lives are ruled by our own needs and desires. But when we can take a step back from our lives, we discover just how often Spirit puts us in a position to show up in service to someone else. While I do this every day professionally, it always amazes me when it happens outside of my office. What I've discovered is that when I give with no strings attached, someone inevitably extends a hand to me the next time I need one. Spirit reminds me that we receive when and as we should.

How I Use This in My Life: **GIVE MORE TO GET MORE**

I believe in the law of abundance, the idea that the more you give, the more you receive. It's simple: If you want more love in your life, learn to give more love; if you want more joy, spread your joy and light; if you want more respect and appreciation, turn up your respect and appreciation for others, and on and on. This energetic give-and-take creates a continuous flow of abundance that never runs empty. Spirits so often realize once they leave the physical and material world that the amount and quality of what they gave directly affected what they received. Money and financial wealth, they finally recognize, are only symbols of what we energetically give and take. In the end, those who serve the most, receive the most.

Integrate the following affirmations into your daily meditation. When you repeat these affirmations like mantras in your mind, you begin to circulate abundant energy. The universal law of give-and-take really does work like a pendulum swing, and your life reflects when it is in balance.

Mentally repeat or say aloud:

I share my abundance with those in need.

I find ways to give back and pay it forward.

I choose to live generously.

I am grateful for what I receive in return.

In addition to repeating these affirmations, consciously think about one recognizable *act* of generosity you can perform every day, whether it's listening to a friend, helping with homework, or returning a phone call. Turn your generous thoughts into generous acts.

What spirits have shared with me over and over again is that to create abundance, we should give abundantly. One of the easiest ways to do this is by giving and extending to others your unique gifts, passions, and talents. When you serve others by doing what you love to do or what comes naturally and easy to you, you get paid for a job well done. I love this quote by American author Margaret Young who writes about prosperity being an "inside job" because it mirrors so well what I hear from those on the Other Side, "Often people attempt to live their lives backwards: They try to have more things, or more money, in order to do more of what they want so they will be happier." It actually works in reverse. Do more of what you love—give freely of who you are—to have more of what you want.

Signs from the Other Side: YOU ARE THE SOURCE OF YOUR OWN ABUNDANCE

As I sat with Amy, I felt the strong presence of a paternal figure, like a father, grandfather, or uncle, and I clairaudiently heard the name "Raymond."

"That's my grandfather," she said.

"I'm also sensing an animal spirit, a cat, with a name like Lizzard?"

"Izzy, my childhood cat!" she exclaimed.

"They are both acting as your guides," I explained, "and they're showing me the movie *The Horse Whisperer* with Robert Redford. Do you work with horses?"

"That's what I *want* to do," Amy's eyes widened. "I'm finishing up classes to become a vet. Horses are my emphasis."

"Why are these spirits making me feel like you're frustrated? Like you're doubting your path. They're also showing me the number twenty-one. How old are you?"

"Thirty-two."

"Did something significant happen when you were twenty-one? Was that a hard time for you? They're showing me pill bottles, which is usually my sign for an overdose."

Amy looked down into her lap and said quietly, "I attempted suicide."

"Grandpa is saying it wasn't your time to die. Have you considered suicide again lately? He's waving his arms in protest, as if to say stop."

Amy looked at me with sad eyes. "I work so hard, but I'm always struggling financially. I feel taken advantage of a lot, like I'm never fairly compensated for what I do." She looked down again. "Sometimes I *do* want to give up."

Amy's grandfather impressed me with an image of Amy as a young girl, along with a clear sense of a repeated pattern, like a circle going round and round, and I understood this was a lifelong challenge for Amy. She unconsciously projected out into the world that she wasn't valuable and worthy of what she wanted, needed, and deserved—and, as a result, she continued to receive less than she wanted, needed, and deserved.

"This is a pattern you have," I said, "and you can break it now. Your guides are working with you from the Other Side to help you heal your low sense of self-worth and finally be compensated for all that you do. This is a soul lesson you came into this life to learn."

"So how do I 'break the pattern'?" Amy asked.

"Izzy and Grandpa are saying the same thing: You're meant to work with animals as it gives you a sense of joy. It's your true calling. Also, the animals' love toward you further validates the value of your work and your sense of worthiness for making a difference in their lives. Why are they showing me the month of September on a calendar?"

"That's when I finish my classes."

"That's it. Once you start doing the work you're meant to do, and so long as you charge what you are worth," I added, "you'll be taken care of financially and you won't feel taken advantage of ever again."

RECEIVE FINANCIAL ABUNDANCE

Over the years, I've done hundreds, if not thousands, of readings for people who are suffering from money problems, be it debt, mismanagement, or excessive spending, saving, or hoarding money. The reasons for these vary. Perhaps an experience where you mismanaged or lost money left you feeling that you aren't responsible enough to wisely handle money in the future. Maybe you witnessed others using money to manipulate and control people and you fear you'll do the same. Maybe your parents were slaves to their money, always working harder to accumulate more to maintain their expensive lifestyle. Perhaps you grew up in poverty and you live in fear that you'll always have less than what you need. Or the opposite— you didn't grow up struggling, but still your family passed on to you their own beliefs that "money creates corruption and greed" or "debt is just a part of life."

Whatever the details of your particular upbringing or financial situation, until you shift *your* beliefs about money and align your energetic vibration with the abundance of the world, financial wealth will stay out of your reach. Changing our perspectives and beliefs isn't always easy to do, so our guides often step in to help shake us up. They work with our subconscious minds to essentially unlearn what was taught to us in our childhood and nudge us to think for ourselves as adults. In other words, they encourage us to live our own money truth. And what they want us to know is that the universe is infinitely abundant and there is enough for everyone.

Yes, that means there is more than enough for you, too! So have an attitude of gratitude, believe that you are worthy and deserving of an abundant life, and give more to receive more. When you do all three, the universe will shower you with riches.

How I Use This in My Life: MAKE THE SHIFT FROM LACK OF TO ABUNDANCE

Paper money may not be the currency of the spirit world, but it cannot be entirely ignored while we reside on earth. So, how can you experience the monetary abundance you need, want, and deserve in your lifetime? As you integrate any or all of the affirmations below into your daily meditation, you will begin to shift your mind-set from "lack of" toward "abundance."

Mentally repeat or say aloud:

I release my fear of not having enough money.

I am not defined by my bank account.

I let go of any tendency to label money as bad or evil.

I separate any past negative financial situation from my present experience.

I let go of my parents' limiting views of money.

I let go of any conscious or unconscious fear, worry, guilt, or anxiety around money and financial security.

The key to shifting your subconscious mind is to replace your negative beliefs and attitudes with repeated use of new positive affirmations. With dedicated repetition, these affirmations will empower you to a new way of thinking that will shift the amount of abundance you receive.

Mentally repeat or say aloud:

I can depend on myself.

I am worthy of having my needs met and provided for at every moment.

I am responsible with money and choose to spend it wisely.

As I do what I love, plenty of money easily follows.

There is enough to go around for everyone, including me.

I am open to receive the unlimited supply of the universe.

Abundance takes many different forms, and I am open to all creative solutions.

I prosper when my thoughts are rich with positive expectation.

I thank my guides in advance for gifting me with an abundance of blessings and miracles.

If you're a natural born giver like I am, then you understand that receiving can be a big challenge. Not only does it feel unnatural to me—like energy going in the wrong direction—it also challenges me in another way. The act of receiving means I have to let go of some of my control "issues" and trust that others will show up with a giving heart and provide me with the care I need. This can feel scary. What if they don't deliver?

FAMILY REUNIONS

Be on the Receiving End

I once read a woman named Susan whose brother in spirit came through, giving me the impression right off the bat that she was the breadwinner in her household. He quite literally showed me a basket of overflowing bread and made me feel that she was under a great deal of stress. I could *feel* Susan's sense of responsibility and accompanying worry.

"Your brother is also showing me an empty piggy bank."

Her mouth fell open. "Just *yesterday* my son brought me his empty piggy bank and asked me to put pennies in it!"

"I feel like the piggy bank has a dual meaning." It's never my intent to pry into anyone's bank account, but her brother was more or less urging me to do so. "Are you having money concerns or financial stress of some kind?" Again, I sensed that her life was unstable financially and emotionally.

Susan sighed. "Yes, my husband, Matt, is launching a start-up with a partner. It's a great opportunity, but he's having some trouble getting it funded, and I'm worried that it'll be a while before the money pans out."

"And you're not working? Why is your brother showing me an image of you at home alone?"

"I had a great career in finance on Wall Street that allowed me to take care of the family for the past eight years, but I just got laid off and now, Matt's starting this new business and…" Her voice trailed off.

"You're resentful," I finished her sentence. "And you're worried your husband won't come through."

"I don't tell him that," Susan raised an eyebrow, "but, yes, I have my doubts, and some days it feels really scary. I'm not sure what to do."

"Your brother is shaking his head—stop blaming your husband about the money. On a soul level, you chose *this* lesson with this man, to experience the opposite of financial abundance and sit in the discomfort that this brings up for a while. But once you let go of some of your control and fear, the money will flood back into the household." I saw in my mind's eye a roller coaster grid with extreme highs and lows but a safe stop at the end.

Susan still looked doubtful.

"Your brother is showing me the passing of a baton, as if to say that there was divine timing, a reason to you getting laid off when you did. It gives Matt the opportunity to step up into *his* power and take care of the family."

"Can I give him an ultimatum, like a deadline to meet?"

"You can hold him accountable for his part of the deal, sure. But my sense is that this switch of the roles is the wake-up call he needed. Can you trust him to give you what you need? Are you open to receiving his help?"

Susan looked at me with an expression that I recognized in myself. She really did want to receive her husband's help, but she was afraid to trust him to deliver.

So many of us, it seems, are faced with a similar lesson to learn in this life: Believe that you are worthy of and deserve abundance in all things, and then open yourself up to receive it.

ONE OF MY longtime clients, Eileen, who is eighty-two, called me recently for a reading. I was happy to hear from her. It had been a couple of years since our last call. As he often did, Eileen's deceased husband, Bruce, made his presence known by appearing as a flash of light right behind Eileen. He impressed into my mind's eye a single lap around a track, my sign for the passing of a full calendar year. I also clairvoyantly saw the opening of a book, combined with a watch. I put it all together.

"Your husband is saying that within the next year, you will have a new beginning, a new chapter in your life, and that this is the perfect time to start something new."

Eileen confirmed that she would be turning eighty-three in several months and that the reason for the reading was to gain clarity about what she should do next. She'd just returned from a yearlong volunteer assignment with the peace corps (At 82! Go, girl!), and she wasn't sure if she should return.

Bruce practically shouted in my ear, *NO. Your time serving is done.* I knew from our history together that much of Eileen's life work had been to help and serve others, which she had done graciously for nearly her entire life. Now, her husband was saying, it's time to rest and take care of *you*. "He's flashing in my mind a hammock on the beach, as if to say relax."

Eileen smiled hearing this. "I don't know, it feels a little selfish that my purpose from here on out is to simply enjoy life. Shouldn't I do more for others?"

I thought to myself, while serving others *is* our true work to do, Eileen was a bit of an overachiever.

"The insight I'm getting from the Other Side is that your next big life lesson is to learn how to joyfully receive love and care from others. Your husband is communicating clearly to me that you've mastered your lesson in serving. Now it's time for a new beginning, a new chapter in your life where you feel deserving to receive."

I paused for a moment and smiled at what Bruce was showing me. "Your husband is showing me a new romantic love for you."

"Oh, that's crazy," Eileen laughed. "What does *he* know?"

I laughed with her. "Well, now that he's on the Other Side, he can see things you can't yet, and he's clearly showing me you standing arm in arm with another man."

"Hmmm." She thought it over. "I'll sit on that one. Anything else?"

"Something about one of your sons."

"I have four—which one?"

"I get the feeling that there is one who feels especially guilty for not being around or helping much in the past. He's your opposite, in a way, and a big part of his life's work is to learn how to be more selfless and giving—like you."

"That's probably my son John. He recently offered to help me financially if I needed it. His offer did take me by surprise, as he's generally not too generous. It was nice of him, but I said no."

"Bruce is saying, let him help you. This will be a win-win for both of you. It will help him learn how to give and you to learn how to receive."

WE ALL HAVE our own lessons to learn around giving and receiving. Where my tendency is to give too much, acting as an enabler who gets taken advantage of, others are challenged to be more generous and selfless. I've learned through personal experience that when you bypass the lesson to be learned, you can be sure the same type of challenging relationship or situation will resurface in your life somewhere down the road—and, more than likely, it'll be much more difficult the next time around. I reflected on the mistake I'd made with Kat, confusing generosity with self-sacrificing behavior. I could almost feel my guides slap my hand from beyond.

In the past, I've sometimes created distance and backed away from relationships that crossed boundaries and required me to confront an unhealthy pattern in myself. But I couldn't really do that with Kat. She works in my home!

I understood that if I didn't meet the challenge and dig deep to find the courage to confront her, despite my discomfort, I'd continue to be taken advantage of. Kat was serving to remind me that my inclination to look the other way or hide doesn't serve me. I mentally affirmed that once the workday was over and I returned home, I'd stand up for myself and step back into my power.

RECONNECT

checked the time. I still had twenty minutes before my first afternoon reading, so I zipped up my motorcycle jacket and hustled down the street to the closest Starbucks. I imagined a hot chai tea—no cream or vanilla flavoring this time—might give me the afternoon boost of energy I'd hoped to get from my Vega One shake. I set out toward Cherry Creek North, Denver's upscale shopping and fashion center. The air was crisp, so I bundled my favorite starlight blue cashmere scarf around my neck and joined the bustle of shoppers and workers taking a similar break. I noticed that some were chatting easily, but others trudged past me with downturned faces and hands shoved into their jacket pockets. Boy, lots of folks seemed to be in a bad mood!

As I made my way down the street, I became acutely aware of an uncomfortable feeling rise up from my stomach and into my chest. Goose bumps traveled up and down my arms as a sudden whip of wind snuck up from behind. "Where is this unsettling feeling coming from?" I was pretty certain it wasn't coming from within me, since my recent signs of abundance (three in a row—thanks, Dad!) had left me feeling quite hopeful, energetic, and light.

When I've done my part to protect my energy and I still feel pressed upon by strange energy that I can't seem to shake, I take a measured breath and close my eyes, no matter where I am—the coffee shop, waiting at a traffic light, in line at the grocery store. This might seem strange to those watching me, but this is a practice I've been doing for years. I stop in my tracks and ask for clarity.

I got my tea, then slipped outside and leaned up against the side of the building. I took a warm sip, closed my eyes, and focused on the uncomfort-able feeling, a rising of discomfort and unease. I breathed it in and sat with it. Sitting with uncomfortable feelings can be just that—uncomfortable—but I've realized that when I resist and attempt to push them away, they only persist and grow stronger. With my back up against the building, I tried to relax into my unease and identify where I felt it most in my body. When I feel the physical sensation, as I did now, that I'm being squeezed and poked from all sides, I can be pretty sure that the feeling isn't within me but coming from outside of me. I opened my eyes just as a young couple rushed past me out the door, bickering back and forth as they did. As their sharp words lingered in the air around me and felt like they were sticking to me, I gained the clar-ity I was searching for. I was soaking up other people's stuff. Here I go again, acting as the world's biggest sponge.

I tightened the scarf around my neck and began to briskly walk back toward my office, thinking, "Ugh, the real world can feel so heavy"; if I'm not careful, other people's "sticky energy" can really tug on me and bring my own energy down in an instant. In moments like this, when I'm feeling espe-cially sensitive to the energy and mood around me, I slip back into my imag-inary bubble of brilliant white light. As I walked past Burberry's storefront window, showcasing a limby mannequin in a tapered white trench, I imag-ined cinching up a similar coat of protective and insulating light (without the $1,700 price tag!). Ahhh, that ought to do it.

How I Use This in My Life: FROM COVERED TO UNCOVERED

> When chaotic energy is swirling around you, you can take mea-sures to protect yourself from getting caught up in other people's real-life drama and losing your connection to yourself and to Spirit. I know that when I start to feel agitated, foggy, fatigued, and heavy—or like I want to run for the hills and get away from everybody—this is my tip-off that I may be covered with exter-nal energy.
>
> For many years now, I've worked weekly with an energy healer named Ariel, who helps to remove the extra sticky gunk that I

pick up from day to day. She acts like a mechanic for my energetic body and gives me weekly tune-ups to clean and clear my energy and shift it back into balance so that it can flow smoothly.

If you're similarly feeling heavy with no obvious explanation as to why, consider that you may be covered with external energy.

In addition to getting "energetically dressed" every morning (page 55), below are my daily practices for mind, body, and spirit to further create a protective boundary between my energy and the world around me.

Mind: Close your eyes and visualize a large vacuum with a long hose secured to the crown of your head. Turn the vacuum on and imagine the hose sucking up any and all negative and fearful thoughts from your mind. Mentally affirm or say aloud, "I release all the negativity I have taken on." Once you imagine (and sometimes actually feel) that your mind is clear, turn up the power of the hose and visualize it removing any heavy and unwanted feelings from your heart. Sit with this visualization for as long as you need to, until you start to feel lighter and brighter.

Body: Clear your body of sticky energy by soaking in a salt bath, hot tub, or pool for at least 15 minutes. Salt is a mineral with the property to extract, and water is a natural filtering and cleansing element. When combined, they are an effective neutralizer as well as a powerful detoxifying agent. Massage is another great way to release negative energy that can get trapped in our physical vessels if we don't regularly decompress and release them. Simply kicking off your shoes and socks and walking barefoot in the grass also helps to pull negative energy out of your body and ground it in the earth. Finally, as a general daily practice, get plenty of sleep and nourish your body with healthy foods. Poor diet and fatigue weaken your immune system along with your energy, and thereby make you more susceptible to attack or influence from the outside.

Spirit: Essential oils, incense, and smudge sprays are some of my favorite tools for clearing the outside energy around me (see page 194 to learn more about smudge sprays). I use a combination of them throughout the day, especially before and after heavy readings where both the living and the dead express great loss, regrets, or fear. In my world, a grounding scent quickly shifts the energy in the room from heavy to light and bright.

Back in my office with hot chai in hand, I sprayed the room with my Smudge in Spray and lit my candles. I felt the tightening in my stomach and chest begin to ease. I was grateful I'd taken those few minutes on the street to reset and protect my energy. I know from past experience that even the slightest disturbance in my energy field can manifest into a much bigger disruption if it isn't handled right away.

At its worst, an energetic hit from another person or by the outside environment can cause me to lose my balance in the here and now. When I'm really knocked off my center, I'll disconnect from the unseen world. This doesn't happen very often given the frequency with which I interact with the Other Side, but when it does, it can give rise to a feeling of separateness, like I'm trudging through the day as a solitary being, detached from the rest of the world. This is a horribly lonely place to be, and spirits will use my personal frame of reference to help me identify this feeling in clients. I will often pick up on a person's sense of aloneness psychically, feeling it as my own. Sometimes the departed will validate my clairsentience by impressing me with an image of their living loved one curled up in the fetal position, lying alone in a dark room.

It was in my loneliest moments when my grandma Babe reached out as evidence that we are actually not as alone as we sometimes acutely feel. While it is true that we each came into this world alone, and we will leave this world alone, over the years spirits have shown me in meditations and readings that we are all connected to something much bigger than ourselves, our communities, and even our species. We're connected to an unseen force of bright, limitless love. There are many names for this—God, Spirit, Source, the Universe, and the Divine. Call it whatever you like, our departed loved ones know this place well. It's in this wondrous world of oneness where they reside now.

How I Use This in My Life: PRAYER FOR CONNECTION

If I find myself knocked into a disconnected, shaky place, I don't stay there long before I pray for reconnection. I'll take a few quiet moments to say inwardly or out loud to God, my guides, and the departed: "Please extend your infinite cord of love and light energy. Let its current of oneness connect with and flow through me once again." I'll then visualize a magnetic silver cord appearing from the Other Side that I plug in to my heart and that lights me up.

Do you ever feel disconnected from the world outside or around you? Are you surrounded by people but still feel all alone? If so, take pause and understand that you are connected to something much greater than you, and when in doubt, repeat "I am that I am." This simple prayer affirms that you are connected to God, within you, as you, and are never truly alone.

While praying for connection will often begin to shift my feelings of detachment to reconnection, it's a subtle shift at best. Unfortunately, we don't just say the magic words and snap our fingers to be instantly cured of loneliness. I wish it were that easy. Just like anything, this practice requires dedicated repetition, like brushing your teeth, along with an added squeeze of faith. I remind myself that it's my mind that tells me I'm alone. It's the mind that creates shadows, fogs, and veils and then creates the feeling of being separate, fueling so many of our insecurities and fears. But this feeling of separateness is not real. We are never truly disconnected. There always remains a thread that connects us to oneness.

I've had vivid glimpses of what it feels like for the departed to be reconnected to this oneness—including a feeling of absolute relief, freedom, contentment, and inner peace, sort of like walking offstage after a big presentation. Spirits have revealed to me through images, thoughts, and feelings that the afterlife is like returning home after a really long and challenging trip. They've communicated this by using my own frame of reference of traveling fifteen hours on a plane through three time zones with fussy children. When a spirit, exhausted on all levels, reaches the Other Side, it's like collapsing into a warm and welcoming bed for many days of rest, restoration, and rejuvenation. Spirits often refer to a secluded area in the afterlife as a "resting place." As soon as we arrive, we are embraced by our departed loved ones and spirit guides who console, comfort, and wrap us in their unconditional love. Sounds pretty heavenly, doesn't it?

In fact, from everything I've seen, heard, and felt from the departed, heaven is the opposite of loneliness. The feeling simply doesn't exist there. Spirits show me that on the Other Side, there is no duality and therefore no darkness, suffering, separation, and pain. It's a playground of pure joy, love, and peace where we reconnect with one another and with the oneness of God's love and light.

I sometimes suggest to clients who are suffering from piercing loneliness that this may be their "sign" they're disconnected from God. Spirits describe "hell" as a lower level existence characterized by a feeling of separation, where wounded souls, both of the living and the departed, reside until they remember that they're not separate at all, but connected to infinite love and light.

FAMILY REUNIONS

A Connection Lost

When a young male in his early thirties named Joshua came in for a reading, I immediately felt his anxiety and desperation fill the room. When I looked at him, it was like I was looking right *through* him. I could clairvoyantly see his spirit standing to the side of his body, completely detached, and the energy within him was gray and dim. It was as if he'd experienced an internal power outage. His inner light was turned off.

His grandfather in spirit reached across the divide, mentally impressing me with an image of my own father taking his life. This frame of reference was my tip-off that this young man was contemplating or may have already attempted suicide. His grandfather's spirit also flashed in my mind a mental movie of Joshua sitting alone in a running car with the windows up. I said gently, "Your grandfather is making me feel like you want to hurt yourself. Is there any truth to this?"

Joshua dropped his head and began to sob into his hands.

"He's showing me a running car. You're in the driver's seat and he is sitting next to you on the passenger side."

After several moments, Joshua lifted his head and choked out the words, "I sat in my car in the garage and let it run, in hopes of passing out from the carbon monoxide. I wanted to die." He paused and cleared his throat. "But it was like something wouldn't let me do it. I finally turned off the ignition."

"That 'something' was your grandfather. He sat with you and gave you the love and will to live. He was right beside you then, and every day since, he watches over you. He's showing me that since you attempted to take your own life, he's flickered with the lights in your house to get your attention."

"The light bulbs *have* been blowing out around the house, and I couldn't figure out why."

And then right on cue, the lights in my office went off for a second and then flickered back on. We both looked at each other in awe.

"He's here, and he's committed to showing you that you're not alone. He's not ever leaving you."

When I said this, Joshua's whole demeanor brightened. His internal light turned back on as he reconnected with something bigger than himself.

This is what our departed loved ones and guides can do. They have the power to intervene in our lives when we need them most, when we've lost our connection to ourselves or to God. They step in to help us remember that we are not strangers to each other. The love of God connects us all on Earth, and the heavenly realm is ours, in life and in death, where the feeling of loneliness and separateness doesn't exist.

How I Use This in My Life: CREATE COMMUNITY BY CONNECTING

I created this meditation while listening to the song "Guide Us Home" by Bad Actress. The chorus says it all: "Put your faith in your heart. Let it lead you from the start and you will always find your way." When you're feeling disconnected, lonely, or isolated, sit down for a moment and take a few breaths; focus on the beating of your heart. Consider that isolation and disconnection is a creation of your mind, so draw your energy down out of your head and into your heart. Imagine it growing brighter, like a flame blazing from the inside out, and expanding light and love in all directions. Repeat to yourself: "Be the light."

Imagine this light reaching out like rays of sunlight and touching the people in your office, on the street, at the playground, or wherever you spend your days. Imagine that your inner light activates the light in those around you, so that *their* light expands, radiates, and reaches back toward you. Imagine this exchange of light creates collective energy wherever you are, like an electric current. When you can visualize and then naturally *feel* connected to everyone and everything around you, your heart will split open wide and attract the love and light of others in. After all, love is magnetic and infectious. People want to be around those in the glow of love.

After a few minutes in meditation, take a deep cleansing breath and feel your heart open and radiate light. Say inwardly or out loud: "Spirit and guides, thank you for guiding me toward other people with an open, loving heart. I am connected to everything around me—first to myself and to everyone in my life, and then to my departed loved ones, higher guides, and to the oneness of God itself. I am never alone, when I show up and shine."

This meditation takes me right out of my fearful, doubting, anxious mind and drops me into my heart. From there, my energy just naturally shifts upward and becomes brighter and lighter. When you ignite your inner light, it has nowhere else to go but outward. That's how light works; it can't be contained for long. Your light is like a current that can shift the energy of the space around you—higher, brighter, and lighter.

RECONNECT IN THE MOMENT

Now, an afternoon slump in your energy or feeling tired, flat, and uninspired doesn't necessarily indicate disconnection; it may simply be a sign that you're distracted from the present moment. You're caught up in your head, which can lead to its own kind of energetic drain, sense of disconnection, and fatigue. When you find yourself sleepwalking or operating as if on autopilot, you likely only need to wake up to the here and now and bring yourself back to the present moment. The best way I know how to do this is through mindfulness.

Many people I know meditate in an effort to become more "mindful." While I make a practice of meditating daily and find it to be tremendously insightful and soothing, this is not the only path to mindfulness. Meditating, counting your mala beads, and hitting the yoga mat can certainly help to quell the mind, but mindfulness can happen anytime and anywhere. As the Zen mantra goes: "Before enlightenment chop wood, carry water. After enlightenment chop wood, carry water." Meaning, make mindfulness a daily practice. Do it over and over again.

As I experience it, mindfulness happens when I pay more attention to the details of the world around me and to what I'm doing, saying, and *feeling* moment to moment. Not so simple to do. Our world is full of distractions, and we're all moving, working, and doing at lightning speed. I can't tell you how many times I've rushed my kids out the door to get to school or hurried myself off to work. On any given day, I'm guilty of missing what's in front of me because my mind is in constant scheduling mode—the carpool pickups, meetings, errands, and household chores. When I notice (and *when* is the key word) that my mind and attention are elsewhere, I will set an intention to slow down, be still, and breathe into the moment. (A reliable indicator that I'm disconnected, lost in my mind, and numbing out is when I catch myself overeating.) In these instances, I'll ask myself, what do I need to help me slow down in this moment? Maybe I need more alone time, a walk in nature, a salt bath, listening time with a friend, a session with my energy healer, a nourishing meal, or to sit down and write in my journal.

However I am able to detach from my rambling thoughts, free myself of distractions, and "get present" gives me a renewed sense of clarity about my own life by allowing me to tap into my inner knowing, and connect with Spirit. In fact, it's *only* when I'm in a present state of mind that I'm able to receive messages from the Other Side. Downloading guidance and insights from beyond doesn't happen when I'm checking my cell phone, sending a text, dwelling on the past, or daydreaming about the future. I've got to be in the right here and *right now*. The same holds true for you.

How I Use This in My Life: FROM DISTRACTION TO CLARITY

It's not uncommon for me to lose my focus and become distracted by the party in my head. When this happens—and it happens to me at some point nearly every day—I will ask my guides to help shift my fragmented attention and focus me back to the present moment. I will ask: "Guides, help me get out of my head and gain the clarity that's right in front of me. I let go of all fearful, anxious, and painful thoughts that distract me from seeing the truth. Help to open my eyes. Give me the courage to see through any illusions and confront what's real."

Sometimes I will literally *feel* my guides shifting my attention. They will send a shudder up my body, like getting the chills, or I might feel an intense pressure on my crown chakra, the portal between this world and the next. As my endless loop of thoughts begins to quiet and recede, I become focused on what's right in front of me. I can see clearly again! What's remarkable about this 180-degree shift is that nothing changed except my mind.

The more aware and mindful we are, the deeper and more meaningful the day-to-day events in our lives become. My biggest "wow" moments happen when I stop racing from one thing to the next and notice the seemingly ordinary stuff. Things like sunsets, laughter, and a good cup of coffee. The theme song to one of my favorite Broadway musicals, *Rent*, begins like this: "Five hundred twenty-five thousand six hundred minutes . . . How do you measure a year?" I often asked myself: What's *my* measure for a meaningful year? A meaningful day? What's my measure for a meaningful life? What I've concluded is that a meaningful life is a mindful life, where I'm awake to *it all*. Some of the most important moments happen, not on holidays or during vacations, but on a typical day like today.

Spirits echo this sentiment often. They communicate that once they cross over from this life to the next, they finally see what they missed when they were here—the moments we are often too rushed to recognize. Upon reflection and with a broader perspective, they acknowledge how rich their lives were.

Spirits urge the living to connect to the moment, to pause, take notice, and appreciate what they can no longer experience. So today, if only to honor someone who has passed, look, listen, touch, and feel the world around you. At some point, pause between one task and the next, and drink in one small detail of your life as you do your morning coffee or tea. Savor it. And then, close your eyes and say hello to your departed loved ones and thank them for joining you in the moment.

I POPPED IN on Chris. He was eating lunch at his desk.

"That looks delicious," I said, eyeballing his tuna nicoise salad. "Where'd you go?"

"Sunflower Market."

My eyes lit up and a smile spread across my face. "Really—sunflower?"

"What's so funny?" Chris tilted his head and smiled back. "It popped up on Groupon this morning, and I bought us a two-for-one lunch. I was going to surprise you and take you there today, but you said you couldn't get away."

"Would you believe that in my meditation this morning, my guides showed me sunflowers. I think they just used you as the messenger."

While many people might pass this exchange off as just a weird coincidence, given the frequency with which occurrences like this happen in my life, I understood that my guides had used Chris to get my attention. It was a clear wink from the Other Side.

"So, what's the message?"

"Just their way of letting me know that they're with me in this moment."

This is a perfect example of what happens when we're present, awake, and paying attention. We notice the signs. And we're reminded that none of us are ever alone.

CHAPTER 6

YOUR GROUND CREW

As I left Chris's office, I called Becca, one of my best girlfriends in Denver. "Want to meet me for a thirty-minute yoga class after work before I head home to a house full of kids and deal with some nanny drama?" I asked.

Whenever I can budget the time, I'll drop in on a yoga class before heading home for the day. The physical release from a sequence of heated poses helps me to transition from medium mode to real-time mommy mode. It also helps me release stress, pent-up energy, and emotions.

"I need the exercise," I griped. "I'm up a few pounds." And there I went again, spiritual "me" slipping back into the very human "me" who easily becomes distracted by my body.

"Maybe you're pregnant." I could feel Becca smiling on the other end of the line.

Unlike some of my friends who handle me more delicately or even put me on a spiritual pedestal, Becca isn't afraid to tease me or say whatever's on her mind. I appreciate that she directly calls me on my very human stuff, even when I don't want to hear it, and reminds me to maintain my sense of humor.

"Funny," I returned. "You know as well as I do that Chris had a vasectomy ten years ago, and even if he hadn't, we're *done*. Five kids between us is enough, don't you think?"

I didn't say it to Becca, but the possibility that we had added another briefly crossed my mind when I skipped my cycle two months in a row. When I mentioned it to my ob-gyn during my annual exam, she assured me that my irregular cycle was likely the result of a hormonal imbalance. A blood test revealed that my thyroid and cortisol levels were off, so she prescribed medication to balance each.

"Yeah, you do have a full house," she agreed. "I'll meet you at the four o'clock hot yoga class, and we can talk about our new neighbor."

"What's that?" I was curious.

"Jill Marsh is moving into our subdivision."

As soon as I heard her name, a feeling I hadn't experienced in many years rose up in my chest: insecurity. Jill was an old sorority sister. She'd known me at one of the most pivotal times in my life—when I first began communicating with the dead. Understandably, when I started making the claim that my Grandma Babe was talking to me from the Other Side, many of the girls in the sorority house, including Jill, were uncomfortable. They didn't understand how mediumship worked, and they questioned if I was making it all up. I wasn't sure that I wasn't imagining it either. I wondered, was I just deeply depressed? Maybe I was crazy? Why couldn't I just be "normal" like the rest of my sorority sisters?

Throughout that time, I spent many lonely nights praying to be something I wasn't. I didn't want to be labeled a freak, mocked, or dismissed. But as hard as I tried to hide my natural gift—thinking this would protect me from friends, family, and anyone else who might not accept me—Grandma Babe and my guides had a different agenda. They continued to connect with me and heighten my sensitivity to the Other Side until I couldn't hide from or ignore it. The spirits weren't going away! It was like that iconic scene in the 1982 supernatural thriller *Poltergeist* where the haunting voice of the young female actor looks into a static television screen and whispers, "They're here."

Except in my case, the presence of my poltergeist (from German *poltern*, meaning "to make noise," and *geist*, meaning "ghost" or "spirit") wasn't scary at all. Grandma Babe surrounded me with love and unconditional acceptance, until finally my resistance broke down. My soul cried out, *Stop betraying me!* until I finally said, "Okay, I give. I will honor who I am. I will find a way to speak my truth."

I dropped out of the sorority soon after that and set the intention to emotionally detach from my sorority sisters' and other people's opinions of me. Over time, I understood that Jill hadn't judged me; she simply didn't understand the direction my life was taking me, and I released any resentment I had toward her.

Still, hearing her name for the first time in over two decades brought up those old feelings of insecurity. Would she respond to my career the same way she had to my late-night conversations with Grandma Babe? As I slipped into self-doubt, my twenty-year-old self was suddenly interrupted by my much more confident grown adult self: *If she doesn't believe in what I do, so what!* I believe in myself, and there isn't a day where I'm not grateful for and proud of the work I get to do.

I heard myself saying to Becca, "It'll be nice to see Jill again," and I realized that I meant it. And then I sighed, "I just hope Connie doesn't get to her first with her neighborhood gossip."

While I'd moved past it, I hadn't forgotten how another longtime neighbor, Connie, had spoken critically about me when Brian and I separated. After all, a psychic medium can't ignore back-fence talk. Think about the last time you passed by your neighborhood gossip: Though you may not be psychic, didn't you get your own uneasy feeling? An uncomfortable sense that maybe he or she wasn't to be trusted? Because I'm highly intuitive and empathic, not only do I feel the energy of the people, situations, and environment around me, but also I often hear it. This may sound like a clever way to eavesdrop, but believe me, it can be more than I want to hear. On any given day, I work to tune out the opinions and judgments of the people around me.

As much as I wanted to dismiss my feelings about Connie as baseless, I intuitively knew she was untrustworthy. But if I had any doubt, one day my clear knowing was confirmed when a mutual friend called to tell me that she'd run into Connie at a department store and that she hadn't wasted a minute before prattling on about why Brian and I divorced. As most anyone would be when they feel falsely accused and attacked, I was hurt. Where I'm much less affected by the judgments and perceptions of the outside world than I once was, I'm not completely immune.

When I first heard how she had spoken about me, I spent more than a few nights lying in bed fantasizing about how I might verbally retaliate, and I came up with some pretty good zingers. My hurt ego wanted to get back at her by stooping to her level, but before I let her have it, my guides tapped me on the shoulder to remind me: Whatever people say about me, be it positive or negative, doesn't really matter. One of my spiritual mentors, Dr. Wayne W. Dyer, liked to say, "What you think about me is none of my business." Spirits affirm this. What they've shown me is that when we each leave this world, we play judge and jury on ourselves; the opinions and judgments of other people don't weigh in.

My guidance from the Other Side also tells me: *Whenever you seek approval or validation outside yourself, you lose. Take back your light. Take back your power.* Whenever I feel my inner light dimming and like I'm shrinking down, that's my "sign" that I'm seeking approval and validation outside of myself.

So instead of marching down the street to Connie's house to give her a piece of my mind, I focused on growing the light of my spirit within. "Be the light," I repeated in my mind. "Be the brighter person. Step back into your power." I visualized my inner light growing from the inside out and spreading like wildfire. Light travels faster than darkness, after all.

How I Use This in My Life: **MAKE THE SHIFT FROM DIM TO BRIGHT**

While we cannot change someone else's mood or mind, we can inspire a shift within our own. Spirits relay to me that it is our individual responsibility to "lighten up" and then *live* by example. When you stoke your inner light, you can dramatically shift your own energy as well as the collective energy around you.

Take a moment now and consider: What lights me up? Meditation and yoga? Dancing, singing, listening to music? Maybe you're inspired by bright color, the smell of fresh flowers, or a quiet room to read or write. Or perhaps breathing fresh air or a walk with a trusted friend encourages your inner light to shine through? There's no one thing that illuminates all, so tune into what lights and lifts you higher. Remember: You are your own energy source, so takes steps daily to recharge.

As if she could see where my memory had just taken me, Becca said, "Who cares what Connie says? Plus I've already spoken with Jill, and she's really looking forward to reconnecting with you. She's been through an ordeal." Becca paused. "Did you know she lost her son Jackson when he was only two? It was a rare genetic issue that no one was aware of until shortly after his birth. He went through many long and painful surgeries, but he didn't make it. Jill's been trying to get pregnant again ever since. She finally did—and then she recently miscarried at seventeen weeks."

"Oh no, I hadn't known about any of this. That's so heartbreaking, so hard." I instantly felt Jill's pain as my own. I'd miscarried twice before I got pregnant with Sam, and the experience was devastating. And Jill had lost a toddler. I couldn't imagine. I'd been so wrapped up in my own feelings from the past that I didn't tune into Jill's present. Just like that, my defensiveness melted and in its place a swelling of empathy and compassion.

"She's probably going to call you for a reading."

I've worked with a lot of families who have miscarried or lost children, and as a mother, I cannot think of a greater loss. So hard to understand and reconcile. Jill was likely seeking answers and closure, and I also got an intuitive hit that she had an insight to offer me, as well. I wondered if Jill coming back into my life had special timing or significance. I trusted that if it did, the reason why would be revealed to me in time.

MY GROUND CREW

I hung up with Becca feeling gratitude that she was part of my "ground crew." If our Team Spirit is a group of departed loved ones, guides, and enlightened spiritual beings who surround, watch over, and guide us from the Other Side, our ground crew is made up of flesh-and-blood individuals

who similarly surround us in life with voices of support and encouragement. In many instances, our companion soul mates are part of our crew.

We each have more than one soul mate in our lifetime, and many times
these mates are some of our best friends. Our companion soul mates aren't
just our romantic partners; they can be our "besties," those we share a natural connection and affinity with and feel like we've known forever, perhaps in
another lifetime. Spirits confirm that our forever friends will continue to be
by our side eternally, in either a physical or spirit form.

How I Use This in My Life: **WHEN NUDGED, MAKE THE CALL**

There is often a telepathic connection with our companion soul
mates. At times, my best girlfriends and I don't feel like we even
need to use words to communicate or have a conversation. We just
know how the other is feeling or thinking, or what we're about to
say next. Often, I will get a call from a good friend at just the right
time, and I too will often feel when my friends need me. When I
have dreams that a friend is going through turmoil or a challenging time, I always call to check in, and my hunch is rarely wrong.

Our guides nudge us unconsciously to act as messengers of
support to those in need, so when you get an out-of-the-blue
feeling or psychic hit on someone (despite the physical distance
that might be between you), that's your sign to reach out.
Chances are good that your efforts will be validated when your
friend confirms that he or she was craving connection or unconsciously calling out for you in a time of need.

I've known Becca since I was six years old when we met in ballet class in
Omaha. While we were not close companions during our childhood, we
reunited in adulthood, as fate would have it, when she and another close
college friend of mine moved to Denver. The three of us became fast friends
all over again. Our adult connection was instant, and we laughed over how
many of our life experiences closely paralleled one another.

Becca and I discovered, for example, that we'd both married men with similar personalities and we both had two boys close in age. With soul mates, this is pretty normal. To this day, it's often the case that we're going through the same type of situation or life event at the same time. It's become a kind of friendly competition where we'll joke with each other, "It happened to me first!"

Laura, another one of my companion soul mates, acts like a mirror to me. Every time I talk to her, I think I'm talking to myself. We recognize similar qualities within each other that we value and appreciate and that inspire us to develop more within ourselves. I met Laura when I moved to Denver from Los Angeles. Her then boyfriend built and lived in the house that Brian and I eventually bought and moved into, and Laura and I laugh over how we've separately and collectively spent over ten years sleeping in the same bedroom. We're both career women who enjoy our independence, and the majority of our time together is actually spent texting back and forth or leaving voice mails in an effort to coordinate our schedules. We see each other when we can, and neither one of us takes the other's busyness personally. When we finally do get together, our connection is naturally easy, comfortable, and safe.

As my friendships with Becca, Laura, and my college bestie Katie have deepened over the years, so has an unspoken agreement that we'll be there for each other unconditionally. We alternately play the role of teacher and student and exchange an equal amount of give and take and love and support. When I think of the many relationships I've had over the course of my lifetime, there aren't that many where I've felt I've gotten as much as I've given. In fact, I can count on one hand the number of people outside my family that this applies to. *That's* what makes a soul mate friendship so special. These supportive and deep bonds remind us that we are not alone on earth. Our soul mates are here for us, now and always.

Signs from the Other Side: **SOUL MATE**

At a recent group reading in New York City, I connected to a "Michael" who I sensed had died of a drug overdose. I was overcome with a sense of dizziness and intoxication, and in my mind's eye I saw the snap of fingers and the number sequence 1-2-3, which are both my signs for when something happens suddenly and unexpectedly.

"Does anyone know a Michael who abruptly died from something drug or alcohol related? I asked the crowd.

A young girl in the third row began sobbing and tentatively raised her hand. "My friend Michael overdosed two weeks ago."

"Your friend is apologizing over and over again for leaving you. He's wrapping his arms around you as if to say he will love you forever."

She sobbed even harder. "He used to say we were 'forever friends.'"

"He's acknowledging how much you taught him in his young life, and he's joking that he is now the wiser one, with the 'home advantage,' and will help guide you from the Other Side."

She smiled through her tears, saying this sounded exactly like him. I clairvoyantly saw Michael's spirit standing behind her. He placed his hands on her shoulders, my sign for, no matter what, when, or why, *I've got your back.*

MAINTAINING FRIENDSHIPS

I'm grateful to have people in my life who I can call on, mentally and literally. I have friends I've known since childhood, as well as from high school, college, and different places where I've lived. And while I cherish the time I spend with friends, as my life grows busier, I don't always know how to maintain all my friendships. When you're already challenged by the prospect of meeting work and family commitments, how do you stay current with everyone else? I do my best, but there don't seem to be enough hours in the day or days in the week for me to stay connected with all the people who have meant something significant to me over the past four decades. And yet, if I don't make the attempt to stay in touch, I feel like I'm breaking the friend code.

I know many women who, like me, suffer from some degree of friend guilt. Thankfully, my Other Side insight has provided me with some relief. What I've come to understand is quite simple: There's no end to the number of people who have the capacity to love, guide, and support us, but maintaining *all* our relationships at the same time is unnecessary and nearly impossible. Just as it is with our romantic partners, each of us attracts certain people into our life experience at different times based on what we need emotionally, philosophically, intellectually, and spiritually. We continue spending time together until our individual needs change or an important insight, healing, or big life lesson has been learned. If we allow them to, everyone on our life team has the power to influence us, but that influence doesn't necessarily last a lifetime.

When I first moved to Detroit in 2000, and before I'd really understood my intuitive gift or how to offer my insights to people, I met a woman named Victoria who became an instant friend. She wholeheartedly believed in me. Even before I knew it, Victoria was convinced that becoming a medium was my life's purpose, and she pushed me to develop my natural abilities and sensitivity. In fact, she arranged for my first public readings and was my constant cheerleader throughout this new period of my life. I, in turn, encouraged her to develop her own psychic gifts, which she did, and today Victoria is a professional psychic intuitive, as well as a best-selling author of both adult mystery and children's fantasy adventure.

Victoria and I remained really tight for a number of years. And because our friendship and mentorship of one another was so close—she weighed in on each of my career moves and I on hers—she also felt comfortable expressing her opinion about my then new relationship with Brian. Her words were blunt: She said Brian wasn't "Mr. Right" but rather "Mr. Right Now." Ouch. Nothing worse than having a friend be less than enthusiastic about a new love, right? In my case, this common disappointment had a special twist: Because we are both psychic, I could *feel* that she'd picked up on other aspects of my budding relationship that she was holding back.

Like many other women in this situation, I felt defensive of Brian and my choice to be with him. Why couldn't she just like him and be happy for me? But deep down, I worried that Victoria's psychic insights might be right, and knowing this created tension between us. As things with Brian became more serious, the time I spent with Victoria became less and less comfortable. Maybe it was her, maybe it was me, but we drifted apart. I knew it was happening, and I felt bad about it, but somehow I couldn't do a U-turn.

Has this ever happened to you? Your friend can see something clearly that you don't yet want to face, so you don't. As the weeks and months turned into years of distance, I came to understand that our separation in no way discounted her significance in my life. She had given me extra courage and confidence to go public with my ability to connect with the Other Side. She was absolutely what I needed at that particular time in my life, and I feel certain she'd say the same thing about me. Plus, this story has a happy ending. Several years later (in fact, after Brian and I chose to raise our family apart), Victoria and I reconnected. We sat down like big girls and discussed the events that caused us to part in the first place, and with the benefit of some distance and retrospect, we put the past in the past and made peace.

To look at my friendship with Victoria from a spiritual perspective, putting our relationship on ice was inevitable because our work together was done for the time being. We had helped each other grow professionally and no longer required the same things from one another in the same way as before. If it hadn't been hurt feelings about Brian that separated us at that time, it would have been something else, because our next life lesson had to be learned separate from one another.

Spirits remind me that relationships are never one-sided; both people always get something out of the deal. The departed also communicate that throughout our lifetime, we're constantly changing and evolving, and because of this, we often outgrow our friendships—and this doesn't make us bad friends. Nor does it mean that we're unlovable when our friends outgrow us.

Just as family may naturally play a bigger or lesser role in your life at different times—bigger when you're a child, lesser when you go out on your own, then maybe bigger again after a marriage or when you welcome children into your life—friends also naturally move in and out of our lives depending on when we most need them and they need us. And sometimes it may be that, as with Victoria, the "good-bye" will actually be a "see you later."

How I Use This in My Life: **MAKE THE SHIFT FROM LOSS TO GRATITUDE**

If the memory of a friend who's faded from my life surfaces in my mind, instead of sinking in to a place of regret, sadness, or loss, I intentionally transform my feeling into gratitude. Saying the following really helps me:

"I'm grateful for time spent with (NAME) and for all of our shared experiences. I wish (NAME) nothing but the best in all his/her future relationships. As I am willing to allow our paths to go in different directions, I am making room in my life for new relationships to enter in. I trust that the Universe will deliver the right people into my life when I need them most."

FRIENDS ON THE FRINGE

Not all friendships have to end or even take a break. Sometimes the intensity, or proximity, between two people simply fades—you're not at odds nor have you completely disappeared from each other's lives. I call these friends on the fringe.

Take my friend Stacy in West Bloomfield, Michigan. When I lived there, she and I were close girlfriends and saw each other often. But since I've moved to Denver, we probably only talk every three to six months now over the phone. I still consider Stacy a good friend; we've had no falling out, but our involvement in each other's lives has changed. Because we see and speak to each other less often, I consider her a friend on the fringe; yet, when we do spend time together—if I'm traveling to Michigan on business, for example— we instantly reconnect. Because it's always so wonderful to see her, I often give myself a hard time for not staying more connected. Maybe I should make more of an effort? Call more? Visit more?

When I find myself losing hours on Facebook lamenting friendships now on the fringe, I remind myself that the time we spent together is no less significant now that we see each other less, and I trust that I will reconnect with these friends when, and if, we both need to. I'll set the intention: "I will not beat myself up with friend guilt. Divine timing will bring us together when it's meant to be."

How I Use This in My Life: TRUST THAT FRIENDSHIPS HAVE DIVINE TIMING

A perfect example of a friend resurfacing in "divine timing" happened to me this past year. Chris and the kids and I were driving to Aspen for the weekend, and for the three hours we were in the car, Jamie—one of my best friends from high school—kept popping into my mind. Actually, she kept popping up everywhere. "Jamie" was the name of a caller on the morning radio show we were listening to; "Jamie" was the name of the barista at the drive-thru Starbucks; and when we passed a car with the license plate "IBJamin," I acknowledged that these were all clear signs that I should reach out to this friend of mine. I made a mental note to follow up with her soon.

Well, the Universe beat me to it. On the second day we were in Aspen, Chris and I were having lunch alone at an outside cafe when I noticed a tall, beautiful blonde walking down the street. I thought to myself, "That looks a lot like Jamie." Then, I saw three blonde little girls following her, and I realized, "It *is* Jamie!" As it turned out, she and her family were on spring vacation as well, staying literally around the corner from us. While Jamie and I have remained close friends since high school graduation, because she still lives in Omaha, we don't spend much time together unless I go home to visit. As a result, our friendship has been on the fringe for many years.

At the café, I understood that divine timing was at work. We were being drawn back together. I felt claircognitively that Jamie's father, who'd died a year prior, was in fact, behind this particular reunion. I felt his presence as Jamie and I embraced and laughed over our "coincidental" run-in. I also intuitively felt that Jamie was still struggling over his passing and that her dad had crossed our paths so that I could help her navigate through her grief. Our families ended up spending much of the weekend together, and I was grateful for the opportunity to reconnect and offer healing support.

KNOW WHEN TO SAY GOOD-BYE

It can feel disappointing when a friendship shifts or drifts, but it can feel even worse to stay locked into any relationship that doesn't serve or advance you forward. You don't need to be a medium to make managing your energy a high priority. We each ought to be cautious about allowing ourselves to become drawn into relationships that drain our energy and light.

Case in point: a former friend named Lisa. From the moment I laid eyes on her, my mental "Caution" sign started blinking. Her energy felt heavy to me; not harmful, but wearing. I found myself protectively crossing my arms across my chest, psychic body language for keep your distance. But instead of listening to my own intuition—the first impression, physical uneasiness, or mental red flag that indicates this person is no good for you; beware and back away—my mind talked me out of what I was feeling. "Rebecca," it said, "don't be so standoffish, so quick to judge."

Lisa and I were introduced through a mutual client, and we do similar healing work, so in an effort to play nice to a colleague, I ignored my guidance and invited her into my world. Lisa soon confided in me that her life was in trouble—money issues and relationship problems. I started to feel her pull on my energy. My executive assistant warned me, "Don't let her use you for free readings."

While I've had my fair share of so-called friends who really just want my Other Side insights, I felt confident that I could keep a healthy boundary around Lisa. That is, until one day, she left a message for me at the office, frantic for spiritual guidance and telling me she'd be waiting by the phone until I called her back. (Geez, no pressure!) I had a full schedule of readings, so when I hadn't returned her call in a few hours, she dashed off an e-mail asking, "Why are you ignoring me?" She then went on and railed against my "insensitivity" and accused me of judging her. Her words were harsh. A few hours later, I got home and unloaded two heavy armfuls of groceries, only to pick up more insistent messages and two even heavier armfuls of *her* baggage. When I checked in with my intuition and guidance, I could see that her accusations and frustration with me were not about me, but a call for help.

While I empathized with all that Lisa was struggling with, and recognized that what she was projecting onto me was her own fear, pain, and insecurity, I still felt a pang of resentment toward her. Why was she attacking me? If anything, I'd been more than supportive of her. Whenever she called, I listened as she talked about her stuff. *Her* problems. *Her* needs. When I thought about it, our friendship was pretty one-sided. It was always the "Lisa show." She never filled me up, and as a result, the friendship was nothing but draining to me.

So what did I do?

I prayed for guidance. And my guidance told me to be the bigger person and do as children's author R. J. Palacio says: "When given the choice between being right or being kind, choose kind." So I mustered up my compassion and I silently blessed Lisa. I mentally sent her love and a prayer to help ease her pain. Then I called her. As kindly and gently as I could, I told her that the relationship felt draining to me and I needed to pull away. This wasn't an easy conversation to have, but it was the truth of how I was feeling, and I knew I had to honor my truth or I'd continue to feel taken advantage of and energetically zapped.

As you might imagine, Lisa didn't like hearing this. She accused me again of being selfish and uncaring, and as she said these things, I reminded myself that when people behave in a way that feels like a personal attack, their anger or frustration is very rarely about anything we've done. They're just caught up in their own pain, and acting out. Don Miguel Ruiz says in his very quotable book *The Four Agreements:* Don't take anything personally. He wisely writes, "Nothing others do is because of you. What others say and do is a projection of their own reality, their own dream." I knew that Lisa was projecting her wounds onto me, and while I felt empathetic that she was hurting, I wasn't willing to absorb any more of her pain.

After our conversation, I closed my eyes and prayed to my guides: "Help me to learn from this experience so as not to repeat it at some later date. Help me to make the shift from feeling hurt to free."

How I Use This in My Life: MAKE THE MENTAL SHIFT FROM HURT TO FREE

I believe in being up front with people, but sometimes confrontation doesn't work. In situations where a person is unwilling or incapable of hearing you or changing to respectfully meet your needs in the relationship, then sometimes a more effective course of action is to respectfully address the conflict and release hurt feelings through the following mind, body, and spirit approach.

Body: Close your eyes and breathe into your feelings. Ask yourself, "Where in my body am I holding on to anger, hurt, resentment, or pain from another person or from a past situation?" Try to identify where in your body you are holding negative feelings. Are they caught in your throat, creating a tightness in your shoulders, or forming into a ball in the pit of your stomach? This awareness will help you pinpoint where in your physical body you need release. This will begin your healing process.

Mind: Repeat affirmations to trigger emotional release and promote further healing. The best time to do this practice is at night before you drift off to sleep, so that the affirmations can take root in your subconscious mind. Create your own or borrow from these:

- "I allow my fear to surface and release from my mind and body now."
- "I am willing to release any resentment toward myself and others right now."
- "I let go of painful memories of the past that cause me to shut down and guard my heart."

- "I let go of all negative attachments tied to anyone who's hurt or betrayed me."
- "I allow my heart to heal from any pain of the past and expand my capacity to love."
- "All my relationships serve as opportunities to learn and grow in love and compassion."

Spirit: Ask your guides to help you shift from feelings of hurt to feeling free. Visualize yourself standing outside on a beautiful summer day, when suddenly a strong gust of warm wind kicks up around you. Instead of turning away from it, turn toward and face it with welcome and outstretched arms. As the warm air rushes past you, it blows away any and all resentment, painful memories, or hurtful words that have attached to you. Continue this visualization until you feel a shift, and trust that your good intentions and prayers will help resolve the conflict in time.

Signs from the Other Side: **FRIEND OR FOE?**

Sometimes unhealthy relationships draw us in, despite our best attempts to resist them or without even realizing they're bad for us. Because I make a living talking to all kinds of people, I'm confident in saying that most of us will encounter people throughout our lives we need to think carefully about friending. Friendship is a two-way agreement to provide love, support, and guidance. Spirits come through often to advise their living loved ones to rethink relationships where these essential ingredients are missing. It does not serve us to stay in relationships, they warn, where we feel depleted, overpowered, or afraid.

I won't forget the sister who came through from the Other Side with a direct order for her twin: Break up with your best friend of over thirty years, already!

I said to my client, Heather, "Your sister is saying this relationship neither uplifts nor fulfills you, and it's time for you to let go."

Heather said she'd known for many years that this friendship wasn't serving her, but she hadn't had the courage to walk away.

"Your sister is shutting a door, as if she's giving you permission to 'shut the door' and end the friendship."

The departed have shown me how when we fail to separate ourselves from unhealthy relationships that weigh us down, our energy gets knocked off balance. Over time, if we remain in a lopsided state, we run the risk of making even more decisions and choices that don't serve us. So consider: Who do I give my precious energy and attention to?

WHAT IS YOUR RELATIONSHIP TRYING TO TEACH YOU?

On a daily basis, clients come to me who are confused, angry, or suffering from a personal relationship that's fraught with difficulty and they don't know why. In some cases, it's a relationship with a loved one who has passed on, but more often the problem is with someone who is still living. In both situations, what I'm able to do for my clients—and what I strive to do for myself—is explore their conflict from a spiritual perspective, which in turn affects how they resolve the relationship in the real world. I'll ask my departed loved ones and guides for guidance (see "Spirit Guidance for Assessing Friendships" below).

Once we have a better understanding of what others are bringing to the relationship, we can be more thoughtful about who we let into our lives. And in doing so, we can purposefully assemble a "ground crew" that serves us best.

How I Use This in My Life: **SPIRIT GUIDANCE FOR ASSESSING FRIENDSHIPS**

Close your eyes and take two slow, deep breaths. As you relax your mind, become aware of your intuitive senses and ask your departed loved ones and guides to join you.

As you hold your friend's name and/or image in your mind's eye, ask your guides for clarity and guidance: "Is this person helping or hindering me? Is this a true friend? A 'challenge' I can learn from? Or a dead end I should give myself permission to say good-bye to? How is this relationship serving me at this time in my life?"

Sit in stillness while your guides reveal insights, truths, and signs to help direct you forward.

When you feel that you've received the clarity you asked for, thank your guides for their wisdom. Finish your meditation by repeating this prayer: "Please continue to guide me in the direction of people whose energy is loving and supportive and who will positively help me to learn and grow."

MAKING NEW FRIENDS

I've happily discovered that when I follow my guidance, the relationships that best serve me flow into my life. This recently happened when I was introduced to a well-respected, talented woman in my field who was interested in partnering with me on a variety of projects. While I recognized Sarah's credentials as excellent, and I had no doubt she could bring a lot to the table, upon meeting her I felt physical resistance rise up in my body. I took this as an intuitive sign that we wouldn't make the best partners, but to be sure I asked my guides for further validation.

Well, ask and you shall receive. In the weeks to come, every time we made plans to get together and discuss how we might collaborate, something would prohibit our meeting. Between the two of us, we had scheduling conflicts, work deadlines, and even a car that broke down. When my e-mails to her starting bouncing back, I took this as the final sign. I said out loud to my guides, "Okay, I get it!" It was clear that our relationship was not meant to be and that forcing the connection would not be to either of our benefits.

Once I let the relationship "go," another one showed up—Diana, another intuitive and also a client of mine. She and I started running into each other outside the office. Every encounter felt charged with serendipity. We finally both agreed: The Universe is bringing us together! As we began to spend time together, more as friends than colleagues, I recognized that her friendship was exactly what I wanted more of in my life.

Loving and supportive, Diana's huge heart radiates out to everyone and everything she does. She gives and gives, with no strings attached, and showers me with unexpected presents; encouraging and kind words via e-mails and texts out of the blue; generous offers of her tools, resources, and expertise when I'm in need; and regular reminders that she's just a call away if I ever need anything. And though it can be out of my comfort zone to accept this much generosity from another person, receiving from her has been a big lesson to me: If I allow it, all the love and positive energy I send out to others is reflected back to me in equal amounts.

My guidance from the Other Side continues to validate for me that whatever we focus on, we attract, wanted or unwanted. So the key is to turn your thoughts and energy away from unwanted relationships, and instead turn your attention toward the kind of people you *want* to attract into your life. This is how you make room for the supportive and loving relationships you deserve. Once you've created the space, the only thing left to do is *let love in*.

CHAPTER 7

LITTLE ANGELS

On my drive home from yoga class, I began repeating under my breath, "Be the light," as I prepared for my confrontation with Kat. I knew that as soon as I walked in the door, I'd be bombarded by the kids, and so I wouldn't have a chance to talk to Kat until later. Still, as I got closer to the house, I felt a tightening around my throat. I recognized the familiar sign—it was my old fear of speaking up. *Ugh.*

Since I was a child, my throat has been my Achilles' heel, my weakest and most vulnerable spot in my body. When I get a cold or the flu, I become hoarse. When I'm stressed or overly exhausted and fatigued, I experience neck tension. When I suppress what I need, ignore my intuition, or swallow my truth, my body sends me a sign. While I was fully prepared to ask Kat about the Costco receipt, the truth was I'd rather not have this uncomfortable conversation, and this resistance was caught in my throat.

I pulled into the driveway, cut the engine, and inhaled deeply. *Breathe.* Holding my breath is a good indicator that I'm in resistance and reacting from fear, so I took in another deep breath and let it out slowly. I started to feel calmer, grounded, and connected to the present moment, which is the seat of our personal power. "Stand tall," I told myself. "You can do this. You've done it before, and remember what Spirit has shown you: Our more difficult and challenging relationships give us the opportunity to rise above our fears and failings and grow stronger."

Feeling bolstered, I got out of the car and went inside. I wasn't a foot through the back door, though, before I was surrounded by the voices of five kids, one rising above the other, each insisting to be heard. The kids are my priority, so I set the intention right then and there to be 100 percent present for them and to put the Kat dilemma on the back burner, at least for the moment.

Sam pulled on my arm and smiled. "Hi, Mommy, can you play with me in my room?"

"Just a minute, honey."

"Becky, do you want to see my geography project?" Hadley pushed in behind Sam and held up a hand-drawn map of all seven continents.

Jakob cut in. "Hi, Mom. I finished my homework. Can I watch TV?"

"Hold on," I said in my mommy referee voice. "Let me put my things down first and then we'll go from there."

ON ANY GIVEN day, my best intention to remain the cool, calm adult isn't always actualized. Two kids may be arguing and slamming doors, another could be resisting doing homework, and the dog has just had an accident on the floor. I strive to be the best mom and stepmom I can be, but I'd be lying if I said it was easy. Simply the striving can be hard work. Years ago, when I was single and childless, and only responsible for myself, life was a breeze. Boy, how that has changed! When I walk into my house at the end of the day, there is no doubt in my mind that I'm outnumbered; I'm just one woman with very limited energy and patience. Faced with five children under one roof, I have no more "my time," and if I'm not careful, my kids' erratic energy can knock me off balance and sometimes take me down.

When I feel pushed and pulled and on the edge of coming undone, I ask my guides to help me shift my energy from a charged reaction to a more neutral response, where I can calmly address the situation at hand. In fact, I will often ask for help *before* I actually need it. I'm known to say a silent prayer as I walk into the house: "God and guides, help me—I'm going in! Help me rise above any frustration that might emerge and stay connected to my higher, loving self." Prayer is powerful, but even I know that you can't give it *all* to God. I still have to do my part. Before cleaning up the accident on the floor or breaking up sibling quarrels, my principal responsibility is to be present.

How I Use This in My Life: GIVE YOUR KIDS A CHARGE

Children are energetic sponges. They easily soak up the energy around them, so if your mood is overwhelmed and irritated, they'll likely respond by returning that same level of intensity back to you. Likewise, if you put off positive vibes, their mood will eventually shift to match yours.

In my home, I often do a mental exercise where I take a deep breath and then project a powerful blast of positive, loving light on my kids. I sometimes accompany this visualization by holding up both of my hands as I imagine beams of white light blasting from the center of my palms and extending out in their direction. I admit, it looks a little hocus-pocus, and the thirteen-year-old will sometimes roll her eyes at me. But I continue to do it because the practice of projecting light is not a hoax; it really does work! I can honestly feel the transfer of positive energy and light when I focus my intention and attention in this way.

What I've discovered in my own household is that when I'm not present with my kids, if they do not feel my genuine interest and attention, they will protest in any number of ways—sulking, whining, brooding, and throwing tantrums. I witness a similar reaction in the spirit world. Every day, spirits do any number of things to get our attention, but most of us don't notice their presence because we aren't present ourselves. We get so caught up in our heads or with our digital devices that we don't see the signs. It's only when we're present that we can connect with the Other Side. The same holds true with our kids.

When my oldest son, Jakob, turned seven, he started acting out. He refused to clean his room, take a shower, get dressed on time, or do much of anything we asked of him. At first, Brian and I assumed his behavior was a natural result of his age or starting the first grade, but after a few frustrating months of battling with him over everything, it seemed, we surrendered. We didn't know what more we could do, so we sought help from our family therapist. Well, he only met with Jakob twice before he concluded that Jakob didn't need therapy. Jakob didn't demonstrate any kind of behavioral or learning issue, he said; rather, he believed that all Jakob really needed was the full attention of the adults in his life. He gently suggested that Brian and I make more time to "just be" with Jakob. I recall getting the chills when he said this, which often happens when my guides have inspired the message being delivered to me. These words had also come directly *from* Jakob. I was instantly reminded of a moment in our neighborhood park when he'd said to me point-blank: "Mommy, I'm right here. Look at me. Be here now with me."

As hard as it was to admit to myself, I knew the guidance was right. I was often somewhere else—preoccupied with my thoughts, distracted by work, focused on my phone, or engaged in household tasks. I was rarely fully present for Jakob. How frustrating this must feel—to have your parents' fleeting attention.

"Just *be* with your children" is a message that is passed on to me by spirits nearly every day. Our undivided and genuine presence is the greatest gift we can give them. The departed urge us to sit with, listen to, and talk with our children. This is when the most meaningful connections are made. Whether it's for the majority of the day or only a handful of hours or even minutes—just be with your children. When you are, they sense, feel, and appreciate it deeply.

Once Brian and I gave Jakob more of our focused attention, he stopped acting out. It was that automatic. He also became even more helpful, engaged, and confident than before. His transformation served as a profound reminder of my most important responsibility as a parent—to be present—and I silently thanked him for being my little messenger.

How I Use This in My Life: **LEARN YOUR CHILD'S LOVE LANGUAGE**

One of the best parenting moves I ever made was reading *The 5 Love Languages of Children* by Gary Chapman and Ross Campbell. This heartfelt tome helps parents discover how to speak their child's special love language in a way that he or she understands and responds to best. What this book brought into focus for me was how differently my boys crave my love and attention. Sam's needs are play-based. He's constantly dragging me into his room or out to the backyard with a pleading, "Play with me, Mommy." Jakob wants one-on-one time with me, too, but communication is how he feels the most connected. He's happiest to sit next to me on the couch and carry on a casual conversation.

When I'm traveling for work, I can intuitively feel when the boys are missing me. Either I'll have a vivid dream about them or I'll suddenly be overcome with the feeling of their presence followed by a tug on my heart. When I intuitively feel either Sam or Jakob in this way, I know they crave connection with me, so I will try and stop whatever I'm doing and take a few minutes to send them energetic hugs and kisses. I visualize Sam and Jakob wherever they might be—in class, on the playground, or at home with their stepsisters—and I'll energetically wrap my arms around them and squeeze them tight. I'll visualize their hearts filling up with my adoration and love, and I'll ask that their guides and angels help them to feel my love throughout the day.

FAMILY REUNIONS

Your Presence Is Your Present

I was reading a small group when three paternal spirits came through.

"I'm hearing two names," I said. "'Jim' and a name that sounds like 'chip'?"

"Oh my God," said a woman named Amy sitting to my right. "My adoptive father was Kip. He died a few months ago."

"Was it cancer? I'm seeing black spots all over his body, and he's showing me the number seventy-two."

"Yes, it was cancer, but he was only seventy when he died."

"He's saying it was his time to go. There was no need to suffer in his body for two more years nor put his family through any more agony watching him die. Now, he's showing me that his heaven is being out in a boat. Did he love to boat?"

Amy smiled. "That sounds just like him."

"He's with another man. Who is Jim?"

Amy thought for a moment. "Well, my birth father was Jim, but I didn't have much of a relationship with him."

"That doesn't matter. Jim and Kip are both here together with you now. I'm getting the sense that Kip is holding your biological dad accountable for something. He's urging him to stand up."

"Hmmmmm…I don't know?" Amy wondered aloud. "It was Kip who raised me. I really had nothing to do with my dad."

"That's it. Jim is apologizing for not being there for you. Do you have two kids of your own? He's showing me the number two."

"Yes," Amy said, turning to the young woman sitting next to her. "This is my oldest daughter, Julie."

"Your dads are showing me a blue ribbon for first place, as if to say that you are passing a big life test. You are coming in first."

Spirits often come through to congratulate and thank their living loved ones for making better choices than they did in life. In this case, Amy's dads were praising her for her parenting. Where Jim had been absent in her life, Amy was present for her daughters.

"Both of them are so proud of you," I continued. "Your loving attention to your daughters is setting into motion a new and much more healthy parent-child relationship."

"That's good to hear," Amy smiled. "I'm a single mom. It's not easy, and I'm doing the best that I can."

"Both of them are acknowledging that. Now Kip is handing you yellow roses. He is saying this is his sign to you."

Amy and her daughter looked at each other in disbelief, and then

Julie began to cry. "Ever since Julie was a little girl, Kip would bring her yellow roses. It was their special thing."

"And it still is," I said. "He's saying that he will continue to deliver you yellow roses. When they show up out of nowhere, it's his way of saying that he is with both of you, always present and always proud."

BREAKING OLD PATTERNS

Soon after the birth of Jakob, a spirit visited me in a dream that revealed itself as Jacob's spirit guide. It called itself Thumbelina. I didn't have any personal connection to this name, so I researched it and discovered that Thumbelina is a character from a Hans Christian Andersen fairy tale and is also referred to as "Little Tiny." "Well that's interesting," I thought to myself. Jakob's paternal grandfather was nicknamed Tiny. He died before Jakob was born. Was he now showing up as his spirit guide?

My intuitive hunch that Grandpa Tiny was working from the Other Side to support Jakob was validated by Brian's attentiveness toward Jakob. Quite naturally and easily, Brian was a caring and loving new father, quite different from how his own father had parented him. Throughout his childhood, Brian's dad had been emotionally and often physically absent. Going back another generation, his dad's dad (Grandpa Tiny) had also acted removed. It soon became clear to me that Grandpa Tiny was supporting both Jakob *and* Brian to break an unhealthy pattern. By inspiring Brian to develop a loving relationship with Jakob, he was rewriting the past and creating a new father-son dynamic for the present and the future.

Everyone we meet, but especially our parents and our children, present us with opportunities to learn more about ourselves, to be and do better every day. How we were raised—including the traits, beliefs, and attitudes that were handed down from our parents, grandparents, and great-grandparents—so often allows us to overcome personal obstacles later in life, resolve issues, and learn important lessons: acceptance, forgiveness, and resilience, as examples. In the most miraculous of situations, our children can help us heal old family wounds and write, rather than repeat, a new story going forward. What the departed have shared with me is that the dynamic of our parent-child relationships is always spiritual by design. While it is our responsibility as parents to protect, help guide, and teach our children well, our children are often the older souls, who come into this life to support, guide, and teach *us*.

FAMILY REUNIONS

Angelic Messengers

During one public reading, I felt a spirit coming in strong with a clear message for someone in the audience. I asked, "Who is Anne, an older woman who died, with a 'son' who also died?"

A woman in the audience spoke up. "Anne was my mother, and I had a son who died."

"His name starts with the letter J."

"His name was Jason," she confirmed.

"He is here with you, and he's telling me that he wasn't supposed to live past twenty years old. Did he die around that age?"

"He was nineteen," she choked.

"Spirit," I asked, "why did you leave early?"

While I waited for an answer, I explained to the audience, "Some souls leave early because they know they can make a bigger impact and be of higher service working from the Other Side."

After I said that, the spirit of Jason flashed an image of my own brother in my mind. "Do you have other children? I'm seeing a pair."

She nodded again. "Jason has a twin brother."

"Okay, now your mom is talking. She's showing me a sign for suicide. Did she take her own life?"

"Yes."

"She's apologizing. She's sorry she left you on your own. She's showing me that she wasn't really present with you when she was alive. She was ill and distracted by her own pain, but now she and your son Jason are together on the Other Side. They are working hand in hand to help guide you as you raise your remaining son. He needs you to be strong for him right now."

She took a deep breath. "He's been in such a dark place since his brother died. I'm trying, but…" Her voice trailed off. "I'm not in a good place, either."

"I'm feeling strongly that Jason is a very old soul, and his role from the very beginning was to help you break a chain of dysfunction in your family history. Your mother is waving me back, as if to say it goes back many generations."

"Our family has always been broken," she wept. "My grandmother took her life, as well."

"This is hard," I empathized, wanting to assure her, "but Jason is right where he is supposed to be. He will help you heal an entire soul group—generations of family members."

"How in the world can I do that?" she sobbed.

"By not giving up. By staying strong and being an example of resilience for your living son. Jason wants you to trust and have faith in a bigger plan. You are needed here, on earth, to redeem your family's history, and his presence will be with you every step of the way."

LITTLE TEACHERS

People don't happen together by accident. Every family has a reason that's spiritual in nature for coming together however it does, even when it's not clear at the time. When Chris and I first blended our families, I absolutely lacked "spiritual clarity" around my new parenting role. Chris and I both struggled with how involved we should be with each other's kids. After all, my boys already had a father, and Chris's girls had an involved mom. I didn't want to overstep the girls' boundaries, and also because I was concerned (okay, terrified) that they may grow to resent me if I competed for their father's attention, I stepped back before I even stepped forward.

In the early days of our new family, I'd consciously withdraw from Chris in an effort to give the girls more space and time with their dad. I'd suggest to Sam and Jakob that we do something separately, or I might retreat upstairs and away from the family altogether. Where I regarded this as a generous move, Chris didn't like it one bit. He explained that it made him feel torn, as if he had to choose between his girls and me.

One night, after Chris suggested we all play a board game in the downstairs living room, I said, "You all go ahead. I'm going to take a bath." Chris said, "Becky can I talk to you for a minute?" Away from the table and out of earshot from the kids, he said, "Please stop doing this. You're acting like a ghost in this house." I could feel his frustration, but I still felt compelled to create my version of "healthy" distance. Upstairs in the tub, I closed my eyes and put in my earbuds. When I hit 'play,' the first song in my shuffled list was "The Ghost in You" by the Psychedelic Furs. If Chris hadn't already made his point, my guides were crystal clear.

I asked them, "Why am I behaving this way? Why am I putting myself at a distance?" After several moments of sitting in the still water, I received my answer: fear of repeating a painful piece of my personal history. Aha! I didn't want Chris's girls to feel like I was competing for his attention or, worse, monopolizing his time and energy, because this is exactly how I'd felt after my parents divorced. My dad's new girlfriend, Sheila, had an overbearing personality. Whenever she was in the room, I felt shoved to the sidelines, overlooked and ignored, and I quickly became resentful of her and angry at Dad for seemingly choosing her over me. I realized that I was now projecting my old, unhealed stuff onto Hadley, Harper, and Hannah. This was not only unfair but also not necessarily how they felt about me. Once I understood the psychology at work, I dug deep to find the courage to share my experience with the girls.

A few days later, I pulled them aside. I explained how I'd felt in my own home growing up and that my intention was to do things very differently in our home—to give them what I didn't get and set a new pattern into motion. I vowed to honor the special relationship they each had with their dad and also be a present, loving, and supportive member of our new blended family. "That is, if you'll have me," I said. All three girls put their arms around me, and as they did, I felt some of my old wounds begin to heal. The moment truly felt like the marker of a new chapter where I could leave my past behind and move forward with the intention to parent in the present moment.

WE SIGNED UP FOR THIS

When we take accountability for our own hurts and disappointments from the past, and forgo projecting them onto our kids, it's a karmic win-win. Everyone heals. And yet like most women I know who decide to end a marriage or a significant relationship and create something new, I spent many sleepless nights projecting my worries onto my kids. How would our divorce affect them? Would it wreck them? Would they ever adjust? Again, my guidance kicked in when my fear threatened to take over. It reassured me: The kids will be all right. They're strong, flexible, and on an unconscious level, they know exactly what they signed up for. In fact, we all do.

What I've learned from the departed is that before being born, we each received a sneak peek into our childhoods. All of us got a glimpse of our early lives, and we also chose our parents. We agreed to the circumstances and environment we'd be born into, even when conditions would be difficult and preexisting, such as coming into a home with a single parent or a disabled sibling or experiencing the death of a parent at an early age. We also chose ahead of time the parent-child dynamics that would challenge us to grow the most and to learn our greatest life lessons.

FAMILY REUNIONS

Predestined but Still Difficult

I'll never forget the reading I did for a woman named Angela, whose brother Michael died at age forty-five. He came through straight away and mentioned his three living children, who Angela now had custody of, and assured his sister that, in time, they would recover from his passing.

"He's saying that they 'knew the deal' coming into this life, that they'd lose their father early."

"How would they know that?" Angela asked.

"It's called a soul contract. They agreed to their life experience ahead of time. And yet, these are often unconscious contracts, and your nieces and nephew will still need time to make sense of it and to grieve."

"The girls are having a hard time, but my nephew has been acting unusually wise beyond his years," Angela said. "We'll be sitting at the dinner table, and he'll come out with some profound story about life and death."

"Michael is speaking through his oldest son," I said. "He's using him as the messenger to send words of comfort and healing to the other two children."

"I just wish there was something more I could do."

Michael's spirit flashed in my mind a series of snapshots of how his sister could best help his children cope through their grief.

"He's showing me that the youngest sister needs quality time. This will help her to open up about her feelings. The other sister," I laughed as Michael flashed an image of ice cream in my mind, "will need to feel spoiled rotten for a while. Take her out for ice cream, buy her little presents, take her to the movies. It might sound indulgent," I said, "but Michael is saying this is what will help her to feel special and loved in his absence. And finally, the oldest son will continue to want to have deep, meaningful conversations about his dad. He's the most connected to him on the Other Side."

Angela was astounded at this very specific guidance, but agreed that it lined up perfectly with each child's unique personality. She thanked me for the insight.

"Don't thank me," I winked. "Thank your brother. This is all coming from him."

Understanding that our children have chosen us as parents and have signed up ahead of time for their particular childhood experience doesn't mean that we can let ourselves off the hook. We must always consider how our actions and decisions impact our children every day of their lives. We have to be careful, mindful, and considerate of them, and when they're struggling, it is our responsibility and role to honor their needs and help them if we can. Spirits have communicated the message to me many times that while we are not meant to rescue our children from life's experiences, we should help prepare them and stand alongside them as they go through life.

So how do we do this? How do we talk to them, treat them with respect, not overwhelm them with emotional responsibility, but give them space and guidance to make sense of what's going on around them and how they're feeling about it?

HONOR THEIR TRUTH

As a child, I was intuitively tuned in to what was happening around me—most notably my parents' crumbling marriage and my father's deep depression—but when I asked questions or shared my feelings, my parents would often dismiss or deny my experience and what I *knew* and felt. I understand now that they were trying to protect me. Their intentions were good, but I remember feeling so confused that they weren't acknowledging what I was clearly sensing. I wondered, "Are they lying to me?" No child wants to believe that their mother or father is being untruthful, and so I convinced myself that I was untrustworthy. My feelings, my guidance, my intuition weren't reliable.

Did you, too, grow up distrusting and second-guessing your intuition? Did you struggle with parents who acted with good intention but nevertheless withheld, edited, or denied important details because they thought you were "too young"? Spirits advise that we're never too young to hear the truth, or speak our own.

The departed have actively shared that one of the greatest gifts we can give our children is to nurture their intuition and encouragement to trust and follow their hearts. As I've said, our feelings are our best guidance, so by giving our children the freedom to express how they feel and to speak and share openly, we encourage them to operate from their truth. Our work as parents is really just to hold space for them to explore this life within reason and age-appropriate boundaries, and so long as they feel our love, attention, and respect, they will be able to handle most any life situation that challenges them.

How I Use This in My Life: **ENCOURAGE YOUR CHILD TO FEEL**

Spirit is very clear on this: When we give our children permission to feel for themselves—this means not projecting our own feelings onto them or dictating to them how they should react to their experiences in any way—we validate their experience as being real for them. This encourages them to trust and know themselves. Children who learn to rely on themselves grow into confident, capable, and independent adults.

As I do my clients, I encourage my kids to go within and meditate for clarity, direction, and answers. One practice I suggest is a brief guided visualization meditation where they ask themselves, "What am I feeling, and what do I need?" Take the meditation one step further by asking: "Departed loved ones and spirit guides, help me understand this situation. Show me what to do." I've explained the meditation process in this kid-friendly way: "It's like dreaming. Close your eyes, be quiet and still. Ask what you want to know and then let your imagination take over. Wait for feelings, words, pictures, and images to appear. This is how your heart and your guides speak to you."

GIVE YOUR CHILDREN A GLIMPSE OF WHAT COMES NEXT

Another part of ensuring that your children feel heard and validated is by telling them the truth. I know that this can be so, so challenging at times; sharing difficult news and hearing the truth from them in return can be hard on the ears. One area of conversation that I know a lot of parents struggle with is how to talk to their children about death and loss, especially when talking about a loved one who has recently passed. Whether it's in response to an out-of-the-blue question like "Why do people die?" or a question about something specific like "Why did our pet get sick?" or "Why is Grandpa in the hospital?" I appreciate that not every parent is comfortable engaging in this dialogue with their kids.

But I've found that most children aren't at all spooked by the subject. Rather, they're very curious about and insightful on our *before-* and afterlife. Where they might not yet understand *why* death happens, most children generally accept that they're a spirit in a temporary body and an extension of something more, and that when we die, we go back home.

As you might imagine, I speak freely and openly about death and the Other Side with my kids. After all, it's my job. A few years ago, I was invited by Jakob's teacher to talk about what I do on Career Day. After explaining to his classmates what a medium does, I casually asked the class, "Have any of *you* ever felt, heard, or seen a spirit?"

Nearly half of the hands shot up. I then shared the story (with Jakob's permission) of when he was four years old, he woke up in the middle of the night insisting that someone was in the room with him. There wasn't an actual person in his bedroom, but I sensed what Jacob did: the presence of a spirit. I made the conscious decision in that moment to acknowledge Jakob's curiosity and explain to him in his own kid language, what he was likely sensing, seeing, and feeling. I did this not only because of my familiarity with things that go bump in the night, but also because I wanted to validate and encourage his curiosity and sensitivity to the Other Side.

I said to Jakob, "When I was your age, I had many imaginary friends who weren't imaginary at all. They were friendly spirits who are very real and who visit us in our dreams to let us know we're loved, safe, and never alone."

"I think it's Grandpa Shelly," he said with conviction.

"That could also be," I said.

"Will he visit me again?"

"If you'd like him to, just close your eyes and think about him. Tell him you love him and that you'd like to feel his love in return." I explained to

Jakob what I tell my clients: Spirits feel what's in our hearts and hear what we're thinking about most, and they can "talk back" by visiting us in our dreams, dropping into our thoughts, or giving us a strong feeling that they are with us in the room.

I told him, "If you wake up again and feel that Grandpa is with you, his spirit is probably trying to say hello. Acknowledge him. Thank him for protecting you, and he will likely return when you call him again."

As a parent, I actively strive to create an open atmosphere for Jakob and Sam, and now with the girls, to feel safe to ask whatever questions pop into their minds and then encourage them to consider all the many possibilities—about my work, of course, but any other topic as well. Hannah, who is the oldest, isn't satisfied with ambiguity. She wants clear-cut answers and explanations. I won't forget the day she sat me down and interviewed me like a journalist.

"So what happens when we die?" she asked without hesitation. I smiled at her easy confidence.

"Well, the first thing to understand is that when we die, we don't stop existing. Meaning, we continue to be alive. We no longer have our physical bodies, but instead we have a light body, or a spirit body. And that body goes to a very beautiful place where we are greeted by other loved ones who have died, like our grandparents and great-grandparents and even some of our pets that passed away. They are so happy to see us again, and they hold us in their arms and assure us that we are safe and there is nothing to be afraid of."

"Is that heaven?" she continued. "Is God there?"

"Well, people have lots of different ideas of who or what and where God is. What I've been shown is that God isn't a person, but a powerful feeling—the feeling of love and that in heaven this feeling is everywhere. It feels awesome, like the best feeling you've ever had. Spirits tell me that heaven looks a lot like our favorite 'happy' place on earth, like Disneyland or a day off from school."

Hannah laughed at this. "That does sound like heaven."

"It's different for everyone. The spirit of a dad once showed me that his heaven was the Pebble Beach golf course. His family agreed that this was one of his favorite places on earth and that playing golf made him very happy. They liked picturing him there."

"My dad's happy place is the beach," Hannah interjected and then asked, "so how do we get to heaven?"

"Imagine that there's a magical trapdoor on your body that only opens when you die. When it opens, your spirit slips right out."

Hannah made a concerned face.

"Spirits tell me that it happens very fast, and it doesn't hurt at all. In fact, they say it feels really good! As our spirit body slips out of our physical body, it becomes weightless like a balloon."

"Does everyone go to heaven?"

"Most everyone," I hedged. "But not everyone, right away. Think of heaven like school. There are different classrooms like kindergarten through twelfth grade. When you die, your spirit graduates to a new grade. So as long as you were a good student in your lifetime—meaning, you were considerate, generous, grateful, and kind, then you graduate to a higher 'class' in heaven. Make sense?"

"Kind of. So we're basically in school forever?"

I laughed. "We're always learning, yes."

How I Use This in My Life: SPARK YOUR CHILD'S CONNECTION

As parents, we can nurture our children's intuition and connection to the spirit world by validating that what they see, feel, and *know* is real.

Music. Musical notes can match the high vibration of the spirit world, which is why some music can actually *lift* our spirits and put us in a heavenly state of mind. Ever notice how a certain song or a favorite musician can brighten your mood and shift your perspective on your life? Play different types of music for your children until you find something that really speaks to them. By listening, singing, and also dancing together, families can strengthen their spiritual bond and connection to the Other Side.

Nature. So many spirits compare their "heaven" to being out in nature, and they confirm that the positive ions we soak up while spending time outdoors is one of the most effective ways to recharge our energy reserves and connect to our departed loved ones. Take your children hiking, biking, swimming, or walking outdoors to feel the presence of Spirit.

Art. Creative right-brain activities strengthen our intuitive mind, which serves as a bridge to the unseen world. Drawing, painting, sculpting, writing poetry, or any creative activity that encourages our children to freely express themselves strengthens their spiritual connection.

Reading. Like art, reading helps to quiet our thinking mind while simultaneously sparking our intuitive mind. Whether you read to your children or they read to you, choose material that offers words of inspiration and insight. Quiet reading time is a great way to connect deeply with your children.

Animals. Ever notice how children gravitate toward animals? Most children easily bond with animals because they recognize and take comfort in their unconditional love and acceptance (animals are pure spirits). Encourage your children to spend time playing with their pets; if you don't have animals at home, visit a petting zoo or volunteer at an animal shelter. Spending time in the presence of animals can spark their spiritual connection.

Family circle. So many of us lead busy lives, but it's very important to make time to slow down, take a seat, and connect as a family. Consider designating a special time each week where the family comes together—around the kitchen table, on a blanket in the backyard, or on the couch in the living room— where everyone shares one uplifting moment and one challenging situation that popped up during the week. When families can feel safe to open up to each other on an emotional level, they strengthen their spiritual bonds, too.

Spirit guides. Encourage your children to call on their

guides and then check in daily to recount how their presence may have been helpful in their lives. This spiritual practice will build their awareness that they have a "team spirit" available to them as they move through their lives and that they're never alone.

BACK IN REAL-TIME, mommy mode, Sam was still tugging on my arm, Hadley was holding up her geography project, and Jakob was waving the TV remote in the air. I took a deep calming breath just as Kat turned the corner. "Hi Becky," she said. I felt a tightening around my throat. Regrettably, the kids would have to wait. I wanted to be present for them, and I knew I wouldn't be able to do it with the weight of the situation on me.

"Kat, can I speak to you for a minute?" I asked. She followed me into the kitchen and out of earshot of the kids. I handed her the Costco receipt where I'd circled the questionable items and continued, "Can you tell me why you bought these things? I don't remember asking you to, and I haven't seen them around the house either. Did you buy them for . . . yourself?"

Kat took the receipt in her hand and looked at me in stunned silence. Her expression validated my intuitive knowing that she'd been charging personal items to our credit card when she shopped for the household. She dissolved into tears. "I'm sorry."

"You know that's stealing," I said.

"I know," she nodded. "And . . . I'll quit."

Before I had a chance to respond, she quickly gathered her things and abruptly walked out of the kitchen.

Now, it was my turn to be stunned. *That's it?* As I heard her close the front door behind her, I realized she must be hiding much more. My mind scrabbled to understand what had just happened, wondering to what degree Kat had stolen from us, and already thinking about how we would need to reschedule the next few days and beyond without a reliable babysitter. In addition to the inconvenience this situation had created for Chris and me, I felt a deep swell of betrayal and loss.

So now what?

I closed my eyes and asked for guidance. "Guides, help me figure out my next step."

I picked up the receipt from the countertop and looked at it again. That's when I noticed the amount of the total bill: $66.66.

A sign.

I quickly looked up the meaning of 66 and 666 on my Angel Numbers app (yes, there is one, and I refer to it often). For 66, it said: When you're burdened by worries, stress, or fear, it's more difficult to hear your guides' loving help. This is a message for you to spend time in prayer and meditation. And for 666, it said: Your thoughts are too focused on material illusions.

I put the two messages together and understood what my guides were telling me: Forget about the money. Forget about the material stuff she took and pray for clarity. Look for the bigger lesson in this. I took another deep breath and focused on gathering myself so that I could move beyond the moment and into the rest of the evening with my family.

After checking in with each of the kids—helping with homework and asking about their day—I retreated to the living room couch for twenty minutes of quiet meditation. I asked for further guidance and opened up to receive clarity and help. By the time Chris arrived home, I'd gained a new perspective. Kat's sudden departure was a gift, something to be grateful for. Finding the Costco receipt was my guides' way of intervening on my behalf to help me see the truth and clean house of someone who was no longer serving my family and me. Where I'd been overlooking her actions and ignoring my intuition that she was lying to me, my guides stepped in to say, *Open your eyes. Stop enabling. Stop giving your power away!*

When I recognized that Kat had presented me with yet another opportunity to stand up for myself and set boundaries for what I will and will not accept, and was thereby helping me to grow stronger, my anxiety and hurt over what she'd done shifted to gratitude. It really did. And on that note, Hadley came flying down the stairs from her bedroom at the same time I walked into the entryway to meet Chris.

"Hey guys!" she said excitedly. "I was in the shower, and my cell got a random call from this number, 666-666-6666. Weird, right?"

She held up the recent call list for us to see. Sure enough, there it was. The same sign!

I laughed out loud. Hadley was acting as my messenger! Our eleven-year-old—a psychic in her own right—had received what I call a "God dial," where spirits use their high-frequency energy to interfere with our phones. It may sound impossible, but this is a real thing—phone calls and texts from beyond. What we can see and touch in this life is not all there is. The strongest forces are invisible. I'd prayed for clarity and guidance, and Spirit was returning my call.

CHAPTER 8

LOVE ON TOP

As Chris and I turned out all the house lights and headed upstairs at the end of the evening, I was still thinking about Hadley's "God dial" and Kat's sudden leaving. I was confident that the situation had resolved itself the way it was meant to, and I was proud of myself for confronting her and standing up for myself and the needs of my family rather than ignoring my own guidance in an effort to placate, please, and accommodate her. Slowly but surely, I thought, I'm getting this lesson right: Step into your power.

I collapsed on the bed. Chris lay down next to me, and I snuggled up to him. He, too, has helped me recognize and reclaim my innate strength, which is why I call him my rock.

In fact, that's exactly what brought us together.

I may be a psychic and a medium, but as I said before, on the day Brian and I decided to finally end our marriage, I was terrified we'd made a huge mistake. On an intuitive level, I knew it was the right thing to do. We had struggled for many years. We had tried to make it work. Finally, we'd agreed it was time to let go. And yet, fear has a way of convincing you otherwise. From our upstairs bedroom, I watched my husband of over eleven years walk out the front door with several suitcases in hand, and my fear was accompanied by gripping sadness and loss. His leaving felt like the equivalent of a death.

Slumped down in front of my altar, I cried for what felt like forever, and then I prayed. I asked God and my guides to reassure me this was the right decision for me, for my longtime friend and partner, and for our boys. I prayed for peace and healing, and asked my guides and departed loved ones to give me the strength and courage I needed to move forward through the darkness and into the light, to carry on and to feel confident in our decision to part ways. I prayed for help in the months to come with all the practical changes a divorce would mean for both my boys and me. I closed my eyes and slipped into a deep meditative state where, with every breath, I invited in more clarity, peace, and resolve.

Several minutes later, I felt the protective and commanding presence of the archangel Michael hover above my right shoulder. I identified him immediately; he always appears in my mind's eye as a vibrant blue light and often shows up to give me courage in times of fear and doubt. Accompanying him, I could feel the presence of my Team Spirit, the departed loved ones, guides, and enlightened beings I've been calling on for nearly twenty years to help guide me through periods of transition and adjustment. They didn't fail me now. I intensely felt their collective presence surround and hold me. I let in their healing and loving light and breath by breath, my chest opened, and I could feel more air enter my lungs. With each slow and deliberate breath, my fearful thoughts began to recede and in their place I felt safe and secure. Not alone anymore.

At that point, a new guide appeared in my mind's eye and greeted me. He told me his name was Hotei, and I recognized him as the big-bellied "Laughing Buddha" who helps the living increase our sense of happiness and joy. I saw him exactly as he is typically depicted, with mala beads around his neck and an unstoppable smile spread across his face. He handed me a rock and said, *You will know you have made the right decision when someone in your life hands you a rock as a gift.* He then placed a strand of mala beads around my neck and told me that both the beads and the rock would serve as signs in the days to come that I was not alone; I was divinely guided, protected, and loved. *Trust in your guides and your intuitive knowing, and everything will be okay,* he finally said before pulling back his energy and fading away.

I came out of my meditation feeling soothed and at rest, much less wobbly than I did going into it. I got up off the floor, reapplied my mascara, and left for work. On the drive over to the office, I repeated Hotei's words over and over in my mind—trust in your guidance and it'll all be okay.

And for the next six hours, I was okay. I got through all my client readings without crying or curling up into a ball, and I even remembered to eat lunch. Still, at the end of the day, I was drained, tired, and emotionally spent. I just wanted to go home and collapse, except that I had a weekly Kabbalah class to attend. Brian and I had signed up for the classes as a couple, hoping to grow individually and together during our time of struggle. When Brian chose to drop out, I continued on my own. I really enjoyed the class, but I didn't want to go tonight. Hadn't I done enough introspective work for one day?

I was sitting in my car at a red light, fully resigned to head home, but when the light changed to green, I felt strongly urged to turn right and head toward class. I followed my guidance, and when I walked into the classroom fifteen minutes later, the first thing I noticed was a quartz crystal rock sitting on my instructor's desk. I knew I'd never seen it there before, and the image of Buddha handing me a rock in my morning meditation came rushing back into my awareness.

"Why is *this* here?" I asked my instructor with curiosity.

"Oh," she laughed, "this darned old thing has been rolling around in my car for a year, and I finally decided to take it out tonight. Something told me to give it away."

She held it up and offered it to me. "It's yours."

I was astounded. I didn't know what to do or say. The Buddha in my morning meditation had clearly said to me that I would know I'd made the right decision when someone handed me a rock as a gift.

Throughout that evening's lecture, I couldn't stop thinking about the rock. I turned it over and over again in my mind. I was anxious, fidgeting in my chair, and not paying attention to a word my instructor was saying. My friend and fellow classmate Chris had forgotten to bring his textbook, so he'd asked me if he could pull his chair over and read from mine. After class was over, he faced me and asked me pointedly, "Are you okay?"

Had it been that obvious?

"I'm okay." I tried to smile, and then I started to cry.

Chris reached his arm out to steady me and said, "This is going to sound really strange, but driving over here tonight, I got the strong sense that I should protect you. I'm not sure from what or why, but it's a strong feeling I have."

As he said the word *protect*, I felt the presence of archangel Michael's protective force surround me again, the same energy from earlier in the day. I thought to myself, "My angels and guides are encouraging Chris to help guide me through this dark and difficult day." And then something else: I noticed Chris was wearing a set of mala prayer beads around his neck.

"Where'd you get *those?*" I now asked, stupefied.

"Don't you remember?" Chris asked. "They were yours. Last year, when you did a reading for me, you said your guides inspired you to give them to me. I've been wearing them ever since."

I hardly remembered the exchange he referenced, but I suddenly sensed that the scene and the conversation we were having was being orchestrated from beyond. "This is *too* weird," I laughed through tears, and shared with Chris the details of my meditation where the Buddha gave me a rock and a set of prayer beads.

Chris smiled. "Makes perfect sense to me. Since I was a baby, my family nicknamed me Happy Buddha."

A rock, a set of prayer beads, and a Happy Buddha. *Really?*

Where I had struggled with doubts earlier in the day over Brian's and my decision to divorce, there could be none now. I'd prayed for clarity and resolve, and my guides had answered my call. They told me to look for the signs, and now here they were. I looked at my friend holding out his hand to steady me, and my intuition told me to take hold of it.

After that fateful evening, it became increasingly clear to me that the Universe had conspired to bring Chris and I together. We already knew each other as friends from the neighborhood, but it wasn't until we started spending one-on-one time together that we began to experience an exponentially high amount of soul mate moments, like where we'd finish each other's thoughts and sentences along with shared déjà vu flashbacks and prophetic dreams that indicated we knew each other in another life. There were many signs that pointed us toward each other, but the icing on the cake was when I recognized that Chris stood solid on his own two feet. Instead of looking to me to be his source of strength, Chris relied on the same support system I do to feel uplifted and fulfilled—that connection to *something bigger*. When I realized this, I understood why he'd stepped into my life when he did. On a spiritual level, we were drinking the same yerbe mate tea; we were matched! And on a human level, he would help me break my lifelong pattern of giving my power away. How? Because Chris didn't need me to feel accepted, happy, healed, or whole. He'd already gotten there on his own.

I was finally able to embrace what the departed have communicated to me for years: In our relationships—to our children, closest friends, parents, spouses, and life partners—it is not our role, our responsibility, or our work to serve as the ultimate source or resource for anyone else. While we can each show up, provide space, and lovingly support and have compassion for the people in our lives, we cannot heal them. We cannot resolve their pain or discontent. We cannot fix or change our partners, nor should we try and manipulate or control them. Furthermore, we cannot give to our partners what they may desperately need and want most—infinite love and acceptance, the kind that heals all wounds and is only found within.

Signs from the Other Side: HEALING OTHERS IS NOT YOUR WORK TO DO

When I think about the importance of supporting ourselves rather than asking others to do that work for us, I recall a small group reading where a father's spirit came through for his son. Using my sense of clear seeing, he validated that his son had recently split from his wife of many years. In my mind's eye, I saw two people being physically torn apart. I also felt that the guilt was weighing heavy on my client.

I said to him, "Dad is saying that it's been a long, drawn-out struggle for you. He's showing me the number three, as if to say the last three years have been hard on you and the relationship."

He nodded that this was true.

"Dad is saying it's not your job to fix this. You did what you could, but your wife was very unhappy."

I paused as this spirit flashed in my mind a series of personal memories from when I worked as a bartender in college—excessive drinking, slurry arguments, and fights. I asked, "Does she have a drinking problem? I'm feeling like she is full of rage, and she would often take it out on you."

"She did," he whispered sadly.

"Your dad is saying to let go of the responsibility to save her, to heal her. Recovery and healing is *her* work, and not yours to do." I added, "When you let go of your obligation to heal her, you will begin to heal yourself."

We each only hold the power to heal and love ourselves, to make ourselves whole and complete. My brother and rabbi, Baruch HaLevi, says about relationships that two halves don't make a whole. Two halves make two half people trying to each fill their own void, or sense of lack, by marrying another "half." But two half people, even together, will often compete for each other's love, attention, and respect in an attempt to feel unconditionally loved, attended to, and respected. Neither person feels fulfilled in this way, and the attempt to beg, borrow, and steal from our partners can be ultimately draining and destructive to the relationship.

Baruch describes the perfect marriage as the coming together of two whole individuals to create something greater than the sum of their parts— something magical and divine. When Chris and I got married, Baruch wrote us a beautiful letter that reminded me of this important truth. He thanked Chris for "stepping into my sister's life and offering her as much as you have received."

Baruch has described exactly what most of us desire: a union of giving and receiving love in perfect balance, where our partner is our equal, where we walk side by side and not in front or behind—a whole individual who can match our light by shining his or her own and who understands that no person, place, or external source can fill him or her up with the infinite love, safety, and belonging we all seek. That filling station is located internally and is connected to the one true source: God.

CHOOSE CAREFULLY

Our choices are powerful and determine the quality of our lives. Every day, we have a choice about whom we want to invest in, commit to, and spend time with. This is especially true with our marriage or life partner. When we choose to stay in our current relationship, it is our responsibility to do our part to really stand up and *show up*—that is, do our own work to love ourselves, be solid and whole on our own, to stand in the center of our own light, and encourage our partner to shine their own light. Each of us is only responsible for doing our part, and we can only hope that our partners show up and do theirs.

ONE OF MY FAVORITE TOOLS

Show Up and Shine

Are you someone who tries to rescue, "fix," and heal others? Someone who uses all of your light to light up those around you? Or relies on your partner to fill *you* up? The next time you feel urged or obligated to do this, recognize that this is not your or your partner's work to do. You cannot fix another person's holes; you cannot make another person whole. Nor can anyone else complete you. What spirits have relayed to me is that it is each of our own responsibilities to fill our self with the love, light, and the strength of God and then show up and shine.

My guides have provided me with a simple visualization that I share with couples seeking to build a relationship of reciprocal give-and-take. In meditation, draw in your mind's eye an illuminated capital *H*, where you are one of the bright pillars and your partner is the other. The horizontal line in the middle connects you both, heart to heart, with reciprocal love, respect, and support. It runs like an energetic current back and forth, connecting you as two whole people, creating something bigger than yourselves.

Admitting to ourselves that our partner may not be our match energetically—perhaps because he or she is not our equal or whole on their own—or that our relationship is draining, dimming, or off course and we're in too deep to correct it can be a terrifying realization. Because I know a thing or two about suppressing or swallowing the truth, I can easily recognize when a friend or client is similarly caught in a spiritual stranglehold. I understand that for those of us who are challenged to speak up and confront the truth, we must absolutely break our silence and release what's inside. Even at the risk of offending or alienating people. Even at the risk of not being accepted or liked. Even at the risk of losing or bringing to an end our most significant relationships. Finding the courage to clearly state our wants and needs can be one of the most challenging experiences of our lifetimes. And yet, cutting the cords around our neck can also set us free.

How I Use This in My Life: MAKE THE SHIFT FROM SILENT TO SEEN

Do you have a habit of keeping quiet? A lifelong pattern of silencing your feelings and not giving words to your inner voice? The insight I've gained from the Other Side is that a weakened throat center, or third chakra, is tied to a pattern of shrinking down, playing small, and not speaking up for one reason or another.

This energetic center governs communication and speaking your truth. When unbalanced, you may feel timid, want to hold back, and feel unable to express your thoughts. Physical illnesses or ailments include hyperthyroidism, skin irritations, ear infections, sore throat, inflammations, laryngitis, and back pain.

Check in with your throat center. Ask yourself, "Have I been honoring my feelings and beliefs and speaking my truth? Have I been talking over others or not listening well lately? Have I been feeling shy and afraid to extend my energy in communication with others? Have I been feeling choked up lately, having a difficult time expressing my feelings and emotions? Have I been stuffing down my feelings with food, drink, or other external suppressants?"

If you answered yes to any of these questions, you likely feel a tightness in your throat. Set a daily intention to open and heal your throat chakra by speaking up, if even in small but bigger ways than you are now. Speak from your heart versus your head. Set the intention before you speak to come from a place of love rather than fear. Let go of the outcome and simply be in the present with your words, thoughts, and feelings and trust that they will be received as they are meant to.

My brother, who has guided thousands of people through grief and mourning, says, "There's only one way to deal with the dark void in your life, and that is to admit it with words, face it with speech, and move through it with communication. Talking about it with your spouse, your children, your parents, your siblings, your family, your friends, your pastor, priest, rabbi, or guru—that is how darkness is dispelled." The key is to talk, to share, to express, to let it out; and as you open up, you simultaneously make the shift from silent to seen.

FAMILY REUNIONS

Speaking the Truth

A client and friend of mine, Ann, was unhappy in her marriage to Paul for years. She loved her husband as a partner to their two boys, but as she started waking up spiritually over the course of several years, she realized they were growing in different directions.

Ann couldn't find the courage to speak this truth to Paul. She didn't want to hurt him, and she was frightened of the unknown—what would her life look like without him? She stuffed down her feelings of discontent for years because she wasn't able to stomach or digest how they truly made her feel. She finally hit her breaking point when she was diagnosed with irritable bowel syndrome. In a reading with Ann, her guides showed me that her emotional stress had manifested into a physical ailment, and the best treatment plan was to finally dislodge her true feelings and speak them out loud. Ann recognized that staying in a state of limbo, where she wrestled with "Should I stay or should I go?" was not serving her. It was physically hurting her!

She decided to tell Paul the truth, and while she later told me it was one of the most challenging and anxiety-provoking conversations she'd ever had, she felt liberated. The next time I saw Ann, she was like a different person. Where she used to act guarded and emotionally locked up, she was speaking articulately and expressing herself with new clarity and confidence.

In many cases, our relationships will be worth the time and dedication it may take to work through a challenge. But it does not serve us to stay in any relationship when the bad outweighs the good; when the dynamic becomes a continuous struggle despite our time, energy, and efforts to make it better; when we feel dimmed, depleted, and drained more than we feel lifted up. Spirits advise that when we've made an earnest effort to take accountability for our own patterns and behavior and attempt to do our part to learn, heal, and grow from a relationship's challenges, and our partner fails to do the same—or grows in a different direction—then we are free to leave and move forward on our own and accept that they are free to move forward on their own.

Spirits frequently step in to give their living loved ones permission to end relationships where both people either can no longer actively work on growing into their highest selves or are ignoring the signs that the relationship has run its course.

Signs from the Other Side: SHOULD I STAY OR SHOULD I GO?

Step 1: Take a mental inventory of how you are feeling. Whatever the emotions, let them all come up. Really feel them, even if it's uncomfortable (and if you're struggling in your relationship, it likely will be). The point here is not to feel bad, but to face your feelings and admit the truth to yourself.

Step 2: Trust how you feel. Get out of your head and trust your intuitive guidance. What does it tell you? If you need more information, ask your guides for clear guidance and signs. Ask them to shed more light and clarity on the relationship. Is there a lesson in the struggle to be learned here? What can I, or we, do to heal this pattern? Or, is it time to let go?

Step 3: Believe that the answer that will serve you *both* will reveal itself in divine time.

Step 4: Act accordingly. Once you gain clarity and have your answer, act on it. Move forward with grace, respect, and confidence before your mind talks you out of what you intuitively know.

FAMILY REUNIONS

Cutting Cords

I can think of a clear example of someone who was struggling in a relationship that was no longer lifting her up, but who wasn't following her guidance to let go. Kris is a therapist whose professional work is to counsel people on being happy in their relationships. When she sat down on my couch, her father's spirit came through with the personality of a drill sergeant.

"Dad isn't wasting any time," I said. "He's showing me the movie *Unfaithful* with Richard Gere and Diane Lane. I may be off here," I said hesitantly, "but I get the feeling that your husband has been… unfaithful."

Kris began to tear up. "Multiple times."

"Dad is acknowledging your feelings of betrayal. He's also impressing me with feelings of disappointment and sadness."

"I'll never trust another man," Kris stammered.

I sensed that Kris was holding on to a lot of hurt feelings that were draining her.

"Dad is saying you must let go of the past to let your life begin again." In my mind's eye, her father's spirit showed me a long rope where her husband was at one end and Kris was at the other. The words of the fable "The Bridge" also flashed in my mind, a sign that spirits use often to communicate this tug-of-war struggle. In the fable, a man on a bridge is tricked into being tied to a stranger hanging by a rope. After many hours, the man cries down to the stranger, "I cannot hold you … and I don't think I can hang on much longer either."

He begs the stranger to try to shimmy his way up the rope and promises to hold on while the stranger does so, but the stranger refuses; he will do nothing to help himself. Eventually, the man holding the rope decides that he will not accept this responsibility and tells the man that his life is in his *own* hands. And he drops the rope.

I said, "Your dad is shaking the rope. He wants you to drop it. He wants you to take care of yourself."

"I'm not sure I can let go," Kris admitted.

I've counseled many clients who desire to release and put closure on a relationship with either a departed or living loved one, but struggle to do so. They show up at my office frustrated that they can't seem to "let go," "get past," or "get over" their relationship. When I psychically tune in to them, I typically sense an energetic block or, like in the reading with Kris, a rope or cord wrapped tightly around them created by fear, resentment, guilt, or betrayal. When we hold on to negative feelings toward another person, a past situation, or ourselves, we stagnate and feel weighed down. When I invite in the departed to provide me with more clarity, they will often guide their living loved ones toward forgiveness. This is the key, they say, to unlocking the past and releasing any pain still tied to it. Forgiveness allows you to heal so your life can begin again.

FAMILY REUNIONS

Practicing Forgiveness

During a small group reading, I heard the name "Bill" repeatedly. "Who's Bill?" I asked the six people sitting in my office. "Also, I'm getting something to do with a pet's ashes?" In my mind's eye, I saw the old box of ashes we once had of our dog.

"Oh my God!" a woman exclaimed. "My ex-husband is Bill, and I still have his dog's ashes in my house. Just the other day, I was conflicted about what to do with them, as I don't want them, and yet I don't want to speak to Bill and ask him to come and get them."

"I think your ex-husband's grandmother has something to say about this. Was her name Ruth?" I felt the strong presence of a paternal grandmother and with it, an image of my own Grandma Ruth.

"Yes," she put a hand to her mouth. "That's her. Oh, Ruth, I really loved her."

"Grandma Ruth is your advocate on the Other Side, and she is encouraging you to stand up, as if to say you need to be accountable for your part in the relationship."

"With Bill? No way. I've already done enough." She crossed her arms defensively. "It's his turn."

"Ruth is shaking her head and flashing an image of Jesus in my mind, which is my sign for forgiveness and acceptance."

"She was very religious, so that makes sense."

"Your lesson here is to forgive your ex-husband for whatever happened in the past. Let go of your old hurts and anger, as they are only serving now to hurt you."

"I know you're right," she said less defensively now. "I struggle with forgiving Bill. I'm still so mad at him for so many things—for being hard on me, for failing the kids."

"Ruth wants you to stop pointing fingers at him and be the bigger person. She's encouraging you to call on her for the strength you need to forgive Bill, and yourself, because until you do, you're trapped. Your life cannot move forward."

How I Use This in My Life: **PRACTICING FORGIVENESS**

Close your eyes and take several deep breaths in and out. Become present with your body, feel where there's any tension or stress, and take inventory of what you're feeling. Put your hand on your heart and mentally affirm or say out loud: "I am letting go of all pain, resentment, and hurt I experienced in the past from (another person or a past situation)."

Ask your departed loved ones and guides to help you release all residual pain you're holding on to in your heart, mind, and body. Imagine them lifting all of your hurt feelings off of you to reveal new light and love within.

Then, ask your departed loved ones and guides to help you forgive yourself for the role *you* played in the relationship or situation. Mentally affirm or say out loud: "Help me to forgive myself for how I may have hurt others or contributed to this painful and conflicted situation."

Finally, call upon archangel Michael and ask that his sword of loving light cut through any negatively charged cords that still entangle you and weigh you down. Mentally affirm or say out loud: "Michael, please free me in all directions now."

Once you've forgiven the people in your life and the past situations that have hurt you—and have also taken accountability for *your* actions, reactions, and the choices you made that contributed to your pain—Spirit miraculously steps in and provides you with new opportunities to open your heart again.

FAMILY REUNIONS

Invite in New Love

I remember a reading I did for a man named Kelly who was struggling with moving past the end of his marriage and the recent death of his father. As we talked, a message came through clearly.

"Your dad is here, and he wants to help you find love again," I told him.

"No way," Kelly blurted out. "I'm not ready for another relationship. Not now."

"Maybe not today—but soon. In fact, he's showing me a calendar year, as if to say by the end of the year. And he's really strong on this point, like he doesn't want you to miss this opportunity. He's saying you will meet someone very similar to your ex-wife in certain ways and not to project your fear of the past onto this new woman."

Kelly was still shaking his head.

"Dad is shaking his head yes. He's saying, pray for forgiveness. Ask your guides to help you reopen your heart, and new love will come to you." I paused for a moment while he impressed me with a mental image. "Why is he showing me poppies?"

Kelly drew in a deep breath. "Poppy—that was what I called him. I never called him 'Dad.'"

"And what is the deck of cards?"

Kelly began to tear up. "When he was younger, he made money as a magician. One of the few things I have of his is his favorite deck of cards."

"That will be your sign from him. When you see cards in unexpected places, that is 'Poppy' letting you know he is still with you and he is working with you to let go of your hurt and your fear and to trust in love again."

A month later, Kelly called my office.

"You're not going to believe this," he said and then laughed at himself, "or maybe you will. After our reading, I prayed like you suggested to forgive my ex-wife. I let all of the painful memories and feelings of hurt, betrayal, and anger rise to the surface. I cried. I yelled. I wrote out everything I was feeling to get it off my chest. Then, I prayed to my guides and asked that all of the hurt feelings be lifted from me and to help me find compassion and forgiveness toward my ex and myself."

"Wow," I said. "Great work. You really took the guidance to heart."

"Well, I'll never doubt you again because…I met someone. We really hit it off, but I was still scared of getting into another relationship. For a week, I didn't return her calls or texts."

"So that was it?" I asked.

"I thought that was it, and then just like you said I would, I started to find playing cards in strange places."

"It's your dad's spirit," I said, "encouraging you to—"

"Call her back," Kelly finished my sentence.

"And did you?"

"I finally mustered up the courage to call her, but she called me first and asked me why I'd texted her in the middle of the night with the word *poppy*! I about had a heart attack. I swear I did not send that message!"

"I know who did." I smiled. "Poppy is sending you a clear sign—don't let this one get away!"

This was the validation Kelly needed to finally let go of his grief, forgive the past, and welcome a new, loving relationship into his life.

LOVE. IT'S GONNA FIND YOU.

A line of questioning I get frequently from the living is: How and when will my heart heal? When will it open again? How can I attract my true love?

While forgiveness acts like a key to unlock a closed heart, what the departed advise above *all else* tends to come as a surprise to the living. Your heart will heal by loving yourself first, just as you are, right now. Loving yourself is how you become the complete person that my brother Baruch speaks about—the whole person who matches and complements another person without seeking to absorb or bask in the other's energy and light. Our hearts can open again when we accept, forgive, and love ourselves into wholeness. Remember: No person, place, or external thing can be your ultimate source of acceptance, love, protection, support, healing, peace, or belonging. When we feel an internal void of any of these feelings, and try and fill it with someone else's energy and light or with our drug of choice (self-medicating with food, alcohol, drugs, shopping, TV, social media, etc.) for that temporary high, we ultimately return to feeling empty or incomplete.

External energy sources are unreliable and limited at best. Filling up is our individual work to do, and we can do this daily by having the courage and heart to love ourselves for who we are, as is, right now. We become a whole and complete individual when we allow ourselves to feel worthy of our own love, when we stand in our own light and stand by the choices we make—the path we feel inclined to follow—and when we speak the truth. No matter what. We attract our true love, that person who matches us perfectly, when we first become our own true love.

Instead of seeking someone to fulfill you, return to yourself. Reach deep down inside and find your way back to you. Reconnect with your light, with your beauty, with your spirit within. Connect to the infinite love and light of God that resides within you, as you. Know yourself and be as lovely as you are, and then you won't have to chase a thing. Another "whole" person will magically walk through your door.

Signs from the Other Side: YOU'VE MET YOUR ENERGETIC MATCH

Oscar Wilde said it perfectly: "Be yourself; everyone else is already taken." When we bask in our own light—forgiving, loving, and accepting ourselves for who we are right now—naturally by the law of attraction, you will inevitably cross paths with your perfect energetic match, someone who is also embodying love and radiating their own inner light.

You'll know you've met your energetic match when you feel it. **It feels deep and real.** You feel the connection deeply inside, without any rational or logical explanation. This person adds a depth and richness to your life, and is not someone you feel that you can walk away from easily.

You are in sync with each other's needs and desires. You just get each other. Your connection is often telepathic. You finish each other's thoughts and sentences, and know what the other is feeling without ever speaking about it.

You have frequent experiences of déjà vu. You have a familiar feeling about the person or the circumstances of your meeting, reminding you that on a soul level, your relationship was predestined and you've known each other before.

You're mentally inseparable. Time and space do not serve to separate or diminish your strong energetic bond. You may think of the other person five seconds before they text or call you. Or you may both pick up on something the other is doing in the exact moment, despite not being present together. The experience is similar to the telepathic connection twins often have.

Love and appreciation are constant. Every day, no matter how much time has passed, you feel deep love and appreciation for the other person's presence in your life. You see your relationship as sacred, and you go to great lengths to protect it, nurture it, and grow it over time.

You are transparent with each other, with nothing to hide. You share a deep commitment to honesty, trust, and truth, and you both feel safe being vulnerable and exposed.

James Bay, one of my favorite artists, sings in "Let It Go": "Why don't you be you and I'll be me." The departed are clear that so long as we each, always, shine our own light and speak our truth, we will be accompanied by others who do the same. When we stop abandoning ourselves and accept ourselves, we find that we're never alone again. When I fell deeply, madly, and truly in love with Chris, not only was I falling for all the personality traits that make him uniquely and adorably him, but also I was drawn to his authenticity and transparency, to his commitment to be 100 percent him while he allowed me to be me. I recognized in Chris what I had also come to learn about myself: As individuals we must be both strong and vulnerable, both flawed and solid on our own before the deepest connections with others can be made.

In my relationships today, I strive to keep my heart open, and it feels wonderful. Yet even still, I will catch myself putting the lock and key back in. It's habit. Like I've said before, to the natural giver in me, being on the receiving end feels like energy going the wrong way. I'm more comfortable focusing on the needs of friends, family, and clients, whether they ask me to or not. Add to that, I feel my most vulnerable when I open up to receive love, support, and care from others, so I have to be mindful of falling back into my old defensive pattern of closing off. Even though I know better, I can easily convince myself that I'm safer behind my protective walls.

I'm grateful when Chris calls me on my false thinking. "Let your heart fall back," he'll say. His version of the "trust fall," the popular trust-building exercise for couples, is centered on the heart. "Trust that I will catch it, hold it, and keep it safe."

Learning to trust. It's not so easy, is it? And especially for those of us who have been hurt or heartbroken in the past. About a year into my relationship with Chris, my guides delivered a powerful message to me about trust. It was through a channeled reading, which is when my guides speak directly to me. I'm sharing it with you here because I believe it is a message for us all:

Dear one,

We are proud of you for your courage to let your shield down, take your armor off, and feel the vulnerability of love. You have been alone for so long. It is time to surrender your fear and begin the journey of letting love in. It is safe. It is time to trust again. You are loved. Love surrounds you every day. Open up and receive it.

PUT LOVE ON TOP

Chris and I set the intention from day one in our relationship to "put love on top," meaning we make our relationship and growing the deep well of love within us and between us our top priority. We do this because we've experienced how when we operate from a solid foundation of love, not only do we feel our best and shine our brightest light forth, but also our love filters down to everyone in our lives—our children, friends, family, and colleagues. When I say we've made this practice a priority, it's because it takes daily work. But in the end, it's absolutely worth it.

FAMILY REUNION

Put Love on Top

I once did a reading for a man named David whose wife of many years came through.

"Why am I clairaudiently hearing the song 'Yellow' by Coldplay?"

David gasped. "We played that song at Jenny's funeral service, and our daughter sang along. It was Jenny's favorite song. How would you know that?"

"She's giving me this detail to prove that she's here with you."

David sat forward. "What else does she have to say?"

"I'm seeing cancer and that she died very suddenly."

"It was a brain tumor," he confirmed. "She died four months after being diagnosed."

"Jenny is making me feel a sense of deep regret. Like she left unfinished business behind."

Her spirit flashed the number three plus an image of my son Sam in my mind. "Do you have three children?"

"Yes," David nodded.

"She's using my own frame of reference to make me feel overwhelmed and busy, like you guys couldn't make time for each other because you were so involved with the kids. She's apologizing for letting your marriage slip. She's saying that if she were to have known that she would die so young, she would have spent more quality time with you alone."

David choked up. "I have the same regret about working so much and wishing we'd had more time to spend together like we did in our earlier years. And now it's too late." He began to sob.

"It's not too late. Jenny is showing me that you can learn from this. Right now you have to play both roles of Mom and Dad for your children, but in time and as a reward for all your hard work, a new love will walk into your life." I paused as she downloaded more information into my mind. "Why did she just flash Hawaii in my mind? I'm getting the sense that this is what her heaven looks like."

"That's where we took our honeymoon," David said through tears. "It's how I like to remember us as a couple."

"Remember what that time together felt like. While the love that you shared with Jenny can never be replaced, you will be given the chance to love again. And next time, you will know to make your relationship your top priority."

The departed pass on the message often: At the end of the day, what matters most is love and to make spending time with those we love our highest priority.

Chris and I make a point to carve out "us" time at least one hour a day. Most often this is when we've collapsed in bed, after family dinner, helping with homework assignments, and corralling our five kids into their own rooms. One hour at the end of the day doesn't sound like much, but it can often be all we need to *just be*, to reestablish our connection through talk and touch, and where we're giving and receiving love and support in balance. Believe me, I'll always welcome more time together, but the reality is that we have to work with what we've got. And most of the time, it's enough.

WHEN DISCONNECTION HAPPENS

A few months ago, Chris went away for four days with his girls to Los Angeles. He'd taken the time off from work to have some special one-on-one time with them and to unplug from work. I'd encouraged him to go, but I hadn't expected that during his time away he'd disconnect from me, too. For nearly four days, we went without texts, e-mails, or phone calls. I wasn't worried; Chris often goes "dark" when he's on vacation and especially with the girls. He does this, he says, to be totally present with them. The gift of presence—spending quality time together—is as important to him as it is to me, and his commitment to bond with his daughters makes me appreciate him even more.

Still. Four days! *What about us?*

When we're together, we can easily dial into each other, often picking up on each other's thoughts and feelings without saying a word. And because telepathic energy transcends space and time, when we're physically apart I can still psychically tune in to him. But as it is with our phones and computers, our energetic signals can sometimes get crossed or drop altogether. After four days without connecting, my meddlesome mind began to stir up stories. I reached out with a text: "Are you okay? Where are you?"

When he didn't text me back, I did exactly what I know not to do: I took it personally.

"What happened to putting *our* love on top?" I questioned. "Aren't I important, too?" My anxious, insecure thoughts continued to spin until I was dizzy. An hour later, just as I was about to text him again with another needy message, my guidance told me: take a walk. As I huffed down the street, my inner voice said gently, "Calm down. Chris loves you. This is *your* stuff."

As I made circles around the neighborhood, I considered, "What *was* my stuff?" I tried on different feelings. Do I feel ignored? Unloved? Disrespected? Was I playing a jealous competition game with the girls? While there were pieces of each of these feelings that I could attach to, nothing really fit. And then I got my intuitive hit: I feel abandoned.

I'd fallen into a common relationship trap. I was looking to and relying on Chris to be my one-stop source of connection and love. *Gah!* Even with all my Other Side insight, it can be easy to forget that another person cannot fill me up. That's my work. I'd abandoned myself!

I knew what I had to do. I had to call "home"—that is, turn inward.

I slowed my pace and set the intention to use my walk as a moving meditation where I'd call on the help of my guides, angels, and departed loved ones to connect me back to *me*. I spoke out loud my fears and feelings: "I feel alone. I feel disconnected. I feel scared." As I continued to walk, I slipped into a semi-meditative state where my mind began to quiet down and I could clearly hear my intuitive voice and the wisdom of my guides say: *You are not alone. You are always surrounded and connected to the love within you and to the love of God.* I felt a warm presence wrap around me, softening my fears.

"Please show me a sign," I whispered.

And right on cue, I passed two cars on the street, one parked in front of the other. One had a license plate with the numbers 222, which means "keep the faith," and the other had a sequence of 144, Chris's personal sign. Ha! This was the work of my guides, validating my connection to something deep within and bigger than myself, and also to remind me that Chris loved me, too. I stopped in the middle of the sidewalk and silently blessed him and his choice to be with his daughters.

Not five minutes later, he called me.

"I'm sorry I haven't called until now," he apologized. "We've been so busy, but know that I love and miss you so much."

While I was happy that he'd finally called, and I delighted in his affectionate words, I no longer needed to hear them to feel solid, secure, and whole. I'd gotten there on my own. I was once again standing in the center of my own love and light.

How I Use This in My Life: RECHARGE THE RESERVES

After communicating with the spirit world for over two decades, what I've come to understand is that the living and the dead aren't all that different. We're energetic beings, connected to one another and powered by the greatest source of energy that exists. Whatever you call it—God, Source, Spirit, or big

LOVE—the truth remains the same: Your level of physical, mental, and spiritual energy is dependent on your ability to go inward and connect to your own reserves. Relying on another person (partner, friend, parent, or child) to fill you up not only is unreliable, but also can create unfair expectations that put stress on and drain *their* energy reserves. We must each connect to our own infinite and unlimited energy supply to power us through the day and through our lives.

So try this: Do at least one thing every day that gives you a charge, a spark, a pop of light. Ask yourself: "What would lift, center, calm, or balance me right now? What activity makes me feel light, bright, and energized? What environments bring me joy and bring forth my best self?" When you take time to fill your own energy reserves, you'll feel less alone and you won't feel the need to rely on other people to fill the void or lift you up.

STILL, ASK FOR WHAT YOU NEED

While the most reliable connection of love and support that you can experience is when you go inward and connect within, we must each also maintain our connections with our loved ones to feel solid and grounded in our relationships. What we each need from our partners to feel and stay connected varies from person to person. For some couples, it doesn't take much—just five minutes of uninterrupted time away from social media and our digital devices to take a walk, speak eye-to-eye, or share a cup of coffee can do the trick.

Ask yourself: "What do I need from my partner?" Do you need a regular date night out? More romantic evenings in, where you hire a sitter to put the kids to bed? A few minutes alone first thing in the morning to connect before the day kicks into gear? Shared play on the weekends? (When spirits share what their heaven looks like, 90 percent of the time they will flash in my mind's eye images that communicate a sense of shared play with their loved ones.) Spend some time thinking about what you desire and need. This is important information to have. However it looks for you and yours, challenge yourself to make time together a regular practice. Even when you're overextended with work, children, or other life obligations, setting an intention to "put love on top" will recharge your connection for another day and create joyful memories to draw from in the future.

CHAPTER 9

FULL CIRCLE

Chris and I were still lying collapsed on our bed, finally taking our "us" time. He pulled me in close and let out a long exhale to match mine. "Long day, huh?"

"It has been *a* day," I said.

"Let's just lie here for a moment and let it all sink in."

Even with all that I'd had to confront since this morning, I really felt grateful more than anything. I reflected on the day and all I had to be thankful for—my children, Chris, and my supportive friends, and for the awesome opportunity I get to help people connect with the Other Side, heal, and move forward with their lives.

How I Use This in My Life: **SHIFT INTO GRATITUDE**

Our human minds can find a million things that are wrong with our lives or easily complain about the tiniest of things. We sweat the small stuff. But that's your mind talking. Your spirit doesn't care what weight you are at or whether you're hitting management goals at your job. Your spirit is entirely focused on what is happening in your *heart*. If you consciously set the intention to operate from your heart instead of from your head, it becomes much easier to feel sincere gratitude for all that you have, recognizing the many blessings in your day-to-day life.

I make a practice of taking five minutes at the end of my day to count my blessings, and I encourage you to do the same. Write them down, speak them aloud, or meditate on them and how they make you feel. Pause and recognize all those special people in your life who give you the opportunity to learn profound lessons that grow your soul. Ask your guides to help you to see your life through a spiritual lens, allowing you to appreciate *it all* (not just the good stuff), knowing everything in your life and in your relationships serves a purpose in getting you where you need to be on your journey. At the end of the day, it's our sincere gratitude that brings about more to appreciate and feel grateful for.

The more you do this practice (I recommend daily), the more blessings you'll draw into your life, because the things you *think* about and *focus* on the most have a way of multiplying.

I lay there for another moment in Chris's arms when I remembered the bag in my purse. I sat up and looked down at him.

"What is it?" he asked with curiosity.

I hesitated. "You're probably going to think this is crazy, but Becca talked me into doing something."

He raised his eyebrows.

I leaned over the side of the bed and pulled the white pharmacy bag out of my purse. "After hearing me complain for the hundredth time today about my pants fitting tight and feeling bloated, she bought me a pregnancy test."

Chris looked at me sideways. "Huh?"

"I know. I told her there's no way I can be pregnant. Although with the weight gain, fatigue, and missed periods, you'd think I was. All textbook signs."

"Well then, go on," Chris smiled and shrugged his shoulders. "Take it and then we can confirm what we already know."

"Which is what?"

"Your tummy is just starting to look like mine," Chris smiled and patted his paunch. "It's a thing that happens with couples. Means you're happy."

I rolled my eyes and walked toward the bathroom. "It only takes a few minutes."

I waited for the strip to process and validate what Chris had just implied. I was simply up a few pounds on the scale, most probably due to stress and a few too many sweet treats, and to get over it already. As I held the strip in my hand, I thought back to the intuitive tug I'd had earlier to call my college friend Jill. I'd been early to meet Becca at the yoga studio when I'd dialed her number.

She answered with a warm "Becky," the name that only my closest and oldest friends call me, and I knew that she was receiving me with a welcome heart. Speaking to her again after nearly twenty years felt instantly familiar and comfortable. Any difficult memories I had about her from the past faded away. We talked easily, and once we'd each painted a broad-strokes picture of our lives since college, there was an inevitable lull in our conversation. In that space, I sensed her grief creep in.

"Jill," I offered, "it's really none of my business, but if you'd like me to ask the spirits about the baby you lost, I'd be happy to."

I don't make blind offers like this often, but I could *feel* her pure intention—she wasn't trying to get something from me. She was grieving and confused. She'd lost her two-year-old to a rare genetic issue and then, after many years of trying to get pregnant again, she had, only to miscarry at seventeen weeks.

"I just want to understand why I lost another child," she said sadly. "I don't know what to do next. Should I try again?"

I wanted to help her, so I asked for clarity.

"Spirit, what message do you have for Jill?"

Quite instantly, I sensed the presence of a grandmother figure. "Is your grandma still alive?"

"No, she died five years after we graduated from college," Jill said.

"She's here, and her spirit is strong. She's showing me feathers as a sign to you. And she's rocking a baby in her arms. An angelic baby spirit."

Jill started to cry. "The baby I just lost?"

"This feels like the spirit of someone else," I said. "I'm also feeling the presence of a young male child. I think this is the spirit of your two-year-old who died."

"Jackson?" she choked.

"Yes. He's jumping up and down. He's so happy he has your attention. He's with your grandmother and the baby. He's saying that he wants you to have another."

"Another? What do you mean?"

"Jackson is saying that he is with another spirit that wants to be born—the baby in your grandmother's arms. He will send her to you when you're ready."

"Her?"

"This baby is a girl."

"A girl," Jill said longingly. "Are you sure?"

"Yes, he is definitely showing me a girl," I smiled through the phone. "Jackson is saying, keep the faith and she will come."

As I recalled this happy look into the future with Jill, I wondered if this baby girl spirit was the *same* spirit that had nudged me awake this very morning? And several mornings before that? Often a repeat visit is an indication that a spirit is anticipating a near-future encounter between me and their living loved one. Had this spirit been following me around in anticipation of my reunion with Jill? That would make sense! A constant reminder I receive from spirits and my guides is that through trust, faith, and by getting out of our own way, many of the details, events, and people in our lives come full circle.

I was so focused on connecting the dots that I almost forgot the pregnancy test in my hands. I looked down at two distinct lines that had appeared on the strip. I felt my breath catch in my throat. Huh? *That can't be right.* I fumbled around in the package and opened another strip. Another minute later, I was staring at two processed strips, and the results were the same.

"No possible way," I whispered under my breath.

Dumbfounded, I walked back into the bedroom and held both positive strips out for Chris to see. "You know what this means?" I suddenly felt wobbly and fell to my knees.

"Becky, what is it?" Chris asked.

"I'm pregnant."

We stared at each other in disbelief for what felt like a very long time. Finally, Chris said, "How? I've been sterile for ten years. If there's something you need to tell me—"

"I can assure you there's been no one else, so it's either you or the Immaculate Conception," I shot back.

Two months ago, when I'd had my annual ob-gyn appointment, I complained about feeling fatigued, bloated, moody, and sometimes nauseous. When I mentioned that I'd missed my cycle twice, my doctor agreed with me that I sounded a lot like a woman who was pregnant. I even joked, "I'm a psychic. You'd think I'd *know* if I was pregnant." But we both dismissed the physical signs since I tend to be irregular anyway and, *ahem*, my husband had a vasectomy ten years ago.

She attributed my slight change in weight and temperament to symptoms of a different kind of hormonal imbalance. She ordered blood work and called me a week later with the results. She confirmed that my thyroid and cortisol levels were high, and the hydrocortisone I'd been taking to treat my adrenal fatigue was likely why I'd missed two menstrual cycles and felt the way I did. She reduced my thyroid medication and told me to stop the hydrocortisone completely. She told me to check back in with her in a couple months to do another round of blood work and to see if my levels had stabilized and were balanced.

So now, here we were two months later with an explanation. I was pregnant.

"What if the tests are wrong?" Chris asked. Granted, two home pregnancy tests were pretty reliable, but I agreed that we had to be certain.

I left a frantic after-hours message with my doctor, and Chris made an appointment with a urology clinic that tests the viability of sperm. Then, I snuck downstairs and called my good friend Laura. I first thought to call Becca—after all, she was the one who talked me into buying the pregnancy test—but I was intuitively nudged to call Laura instead.

When she picked up, I didn't even say hello. "This is a crisis," I whispered out of earshot of Chris. "You're not going to believe this. I'm pregnant."

Laura drew in a breath. I expected her response to mirror mine. Instead, she said, "Becky, this isn't a crisis. It's a *miracle*. It's like when I found out I was pregnant with Brooks."

Laura and her husband, Gregg, had tried for over a year to get pregnant. When she didn't, her fertility doctor suggested she consider adoption. Laura was deeply disappointed but accepted that this may be the only way for her to have a child at age thirty-nine. They began the lengthy adoption process and a year later, as she and Gregg were planning to leave for Russia to bring back their new baby, Laura realized she'd missed a period. After giving up on the possibility, she'd finally gotten pregnant unintentionally. When she called to tell me that she had two babies coming at the same time, I'd similarly said to her, "It's a miracle."

Once again, our lives were playing out on parallel lines. When I thought about it further, I realized I was thirty-nine, too, the same age Laura was when she had her "surprise" pregnancy. Now I understood why I'd intuitively called her first with the news—only she could provide me with this synchronistic perspective.

"This is too weird," I said.

"Well, I'm just going to ask the obvious," Laura said. "Didn't you pick up on this? Of all people, I'd assume you would have received a few signs."

It was a fair question, and I was wondering the same thing. Some kind of psychic medium I am. I thought I was just getting fat. Why hadn't I received any psychic hits or signs from beyond? As I asked myself this question, I intuitively felt something click into place.

"Maybe there was a sign—a big sign—and I misread it," I said. "The spirit of a baby girl has been waking me up in the middle of the night for weeks. Today I thought I'd found her rightful owner but—" I thought back to my reading with Jill. Her departed grandmother had absolutely been rocking a baby girl, Jill's unborn child. But perhaps these spirits weren't one and the same. Perhaps the baby girl spirit who'd been appearing in my bedroom didn't belong to Jill but to *me*.

"A girl?" Laura's voice softened.

Yes, a girl. My mind suddenly flashed back to a trip Chris and I took to New Orleans when we first started dating, to see Pearl Jam play at the Voodoo music festival. The day of the concert, we wandered around the French Quarter and, on a whim, stopped to have our tarot cards read by a woman all dressed in purple who'd set up a table on the street. As she started flipping over cards, she asked me if I had two boys. I nodded that I did. She then said, "You're going to have a third child, and it will be a girl."

I remember looking at Chris and laughing, "No chance, not another one!"

What I meant was, not another *psychic.* Over the years, I've been told by a handful of psychics and other intuitive friends that I'm meant to have a girl, and I've been visited by a little girl with dark hair and blue eyes in my meditations for years. I'd always known a female soul was somewhere out there claiming to be mine.

But then, like my college friend Jill, I had boys. And after Brian and I divorced, and when Chris told me he'd had a vasectomy, I erased from my mind the chance of having another child—boy or a girl.

That night, I went to sleep with the memory of all these signs swirling around in my head. Could it really be? Was I pregnant? *It was impossible, wasn't it?*

The next day, Chris dropped off a sperm sample at the urology clinic, and while we waited for the results, we drove to one of our favorite restaurants to grab a late lunch. We ate in silence. We were still so dazed and confused. I mean, I know God works in mysterious ways, but this seemed a little over the top. An hour later, the clinic called, and I watched the expression on Chris's face turn from confusion to absolute wonder. He hung up the phone and started to laugh. "I never thought I'd be saying these words again: I can make babies."

Sometimes I think the dead live to play tricks like this on us. As if to say: Nothing's impossible.

FAMILY REUNIONS

A Birthday Surprise

In one of the episodes of *The Last Goodbye,* I traveled to the outer suburbs of San Francisco and met with Wendy and Jason, a brother and sister who'd recently lost their mother.

"Your mother is holding a baby boy. Are you trying to conceive?" I asked Wendy.

"We are."

"Mom is showing me the number seven. I'm getting that this number will factor into his birthday or the date you conceive. The significance of this number will become clear in time, even if it doesn't make sense right now."

Not three weeks later, I received an e-mail from Jason: "I just wanted to confirm that you were 100% correct in what you said; however, the baby boy you saw my mother holding was mine!"

Jason explained that within days after the reading, an ex-girlfriend of his contacted him out of the blue to share with him the unexpected news—he had a son. Not only that, he was born on 7-17 at 12:57 a.m.

"The number 7 is all over his birth," Jason wrote, and just as his mother in spirit had predicted. He confided, "What could be regarded as a huge mistake has been for me the greatest blessing."

This story perfectly illustrates how our lives really do unfold in miraculous ways. As much as we try to predict or control outcomes, we just do not and cannot always know what awaits us around the next turn.

THE STORY OF OUR MIRACLE

Three days later, I lay on an examination table with my slightly swollen belly exposed. The ultrasound technician said, "Okay, let's take a look." She moved the cool, wet wand back and forth until she stopped on my right side. "No question about it. There's your baby," she smiled down at me. "According to my measurements, looks to be seventeen to eighteen weeks along. Very active, too. Moving around all over the place."

I quickly did the mental math in my head. Chris and I looked at each other in stunned disbelief again. *That's over four months?*

"I'm already four months pregnant?" I asked with alarm.

"Yes, and listen to this heartbeat." She turned up a knob on her machine. *Tha-thump, tha-thump.* There it was. Chris squeezed my hand.

"Very strong heartbeat. Do you want to know the gender?"

Chris and I both nodded that we did.

"It's a girl."

I put my hand to my heart and started to cry. A girl. I immediately thought back to a session I'd had with Ariel, my energy healer a few months ago. She'd said she felt a huge wave of energy swirling around my body, almost like confetti in the air, and the sense that something very exciting was about to happen. "A big surprise," she'd called it. "Your guides are standing tall all around you, very excited and eager for you to discover the news." But she couldn't put her finger on what it was exactly. At the time, I'd hoped it was a sign indicating a move to a bigger house.

But no, *this* was the surprise. And a big one it was. I thought about what I so often say to clients who can't seem to understand the navigation of their lives. I tell them: "Stop overthinking and trying to control the details, and instead surrender to the bigger picture coming together behind the scenes." Where I'd written another child off as an impossibility, this baby girl spirit—the one who I'd seen in dreams and meditations and who had been predicted by so many for so long—had finally found a way in. The baby growing inside me brought new meaning to "If there's a will, there's a way." Nothing is impossible. Nor are our lives predictable.

I cradled my belly and looked up at Chris. "For ten years I couldn't make babies," he laughed with tears in his eyes. I squeezed his hand and laughed, too.

In the days and weeks that followed, Chris and I learned that he'd had a "spontaneous reversal" of his vasectomy, when the tubes that were cut reattach to themselves spontaneously. While this can sometimes happen within the first year following the procedure, it is almost unheard of to occur ten years later. According to a reputable Harvard study, spontaneous reversal or recanalization has a 0 to 1 percent chance of occurrence. That's zero to one. So it wasn't quite Immaculate Conception, but Laura was right: that I'd gotten pregnant was nothing short of miraculous.

SOMETHING MUCH BIGGER AT WORK

We each have free will, but what I've learned is that some events in our lives are predestined and inevitable, and they're going to play out no matter what we have to say or think about it. One of my favorite sayings is: If you want to make God laugh, tell him your plans. I'd spent a lot of time and energy making plans for professional projects that would govern the next year of my life—the writing of this book, a possible second season of *The Last Goodbye*, and a demanding nationwide tour schedule, on top of Chris's and my responsibility to our five children. I thought I'd known how the next chapter of our lives would play out—and as so often happens, my plan was not God's plan. I was sure my guides were having a good laugh at this one.

As Chris and I looked at each other in the doctor's office, I had the sense of clear knowing that becoming a mother to this baby was part of life's divine plan for me. I felt a swelling of gratitude and happiness and a deep honor to accept the role.

FAMILY REUNIONS

Some Things Are Meant to Be

Our lives take us in all kinds of unexpected directions, and spirits seem to really enjoy bringing us surprises. One such instance was when I did a reading for a woman named Gwynne. As soon as she sat down, an unusual image popped into my mind.

"Why is Spirit showing me a fiddle?" I asked her. "And the Los Angeles airport?" Neither of these images are "signs" I typically interpret, so I wasn't sure how to put the two together.

"Oh my God, that's where we met." Gwynne then recounted how she'd recently met a man with a fiddle at that airport. "As I stood in line, I felt a tap on my shoulder. I turned my head and there, standing next to me, was a very handsome pilot. He pointed to the case I was carrying and said, 'Hey, what's that?'"

She told him it was a viola and then noticed that he was carrying a similar case; it contained his fiddle. On a whim, she scribbled her name and number on a piece of paper and handed it to him.

"I told him I'd always wanted to learn some fiddle tunes," she explained.

"After he walked away, I felt like I'd been struck by some unseen force."

"I'm getting the feeling this man is a soul mate," I said to Gwynne. I was also sensing her internal conflict. I got the feeling that she was resisting him for some reason. I wondered if the diamond ring on her left hand had something to do with this.

"Our pull toward each other was unmistakable, but it was complicated by the fact that we were *both* married," she confirmed my hunch. "But when a couple of weeks later he called me, we arranged to meet at the airport anyway. There were no words at first. I just leaned on the door of the car and stood frozen until he walked up with a smile on his face and kissed me—like I had never been kissed before."

"My sense is that this was far from something either of you consciously sought," I said, "but that you were both unconsciously looking for each other."

Gwynne nodded that this was true. As much as I don't make it a practice to give people specific marriage advice, I agreed that she really ought to listen to her feelings. "Our feelings are our best guidance, and while we can choose to not act on them, we can't stop them. So as you allow yourself to be honest with how you feel, also ask your departed loved ones and guides for the best direction forward."

Six months later, she returned for a reading and described what her heart told her to do.

"I was terrified and uncertain of the effect leaving my marriage would have on everyone's lives," Gwynne said. "But I knew that I had never really been happy with my husband and that I had always felt an empty space in my heart. I kept this secret for years. I kept it all inside, burying my sadness deeper within me because I thought I could *make* it work. I was living an illusion that, if I did whatever I could to make sure my husband was happy and my kids were happy, then I would somehow be happy. Meanwhile, I was suffering and suffocating inside. I was afraid to admit the truth to myself and to anyone else, for that matter.

"The time had come for me to face my own fears. Two months after my encounter with Joe in the airport, I had an emergency surgery—I believe it was the inevitable result of holding in my unhappiness—and I realized that I couldn't continue to go down the same path. I prayed and asked God and my guides to release me from my fear of ending a 22-year marriage and what that would entail. But as soon as I did, I felt the fear leave my body, and in its place came a feeling of peace. It filled me up and brought me to a still point of knowing exactly what I needed to do.

"It took courage, but today I am married to the love of my life, the one I had been seeking forever. We both followed our intuition, tossing away what everyone else thought or said or advised, and my entire life has shifted."

One of my favorite sayings goes like this: Someday, everything will make perfect sense. So for now, laugh at the confusion, smile through the tears, and keep reminding yourself that everything happens for a reason. Once you begin to recognize that your life has a plan, an order, and a brilliant design, you too may begin to feel an internal shift from fear and resistance to acceptance and peace of the unexpected and unknown.

KEEP THE FAITH

For the next few months after the discovery that I was pregnant, I was on a high over how our lives were unfolding in some kind of magical and unexpected way. Chris and I could hardly keep ourselves from telling anyone who would listen about our "miraculous conception" and how a divine plan was running the course of our lives. But then, in my eighth month of pregnancy, reality, and the baby, started kicking me hard.

Chris was getting ready to leave the house one morning and run the girls to school. Hannah was screaming "Dad, come on!" from the bottom of the stairs, when I emerged from the bathroom with a tear-soaked face. He stopped in his tracks and looked at me with concern.

"What's wrong?"

I burst back into tears. "How are we going to do this?" I cried. "Another baby? *What are we thinking?* I'm starting to stress the details. We're still in limbo with the house, we have both of our jobs to juggle, five kids to carpool to three different schools, and now we're adding a newborn to the mix." Not only did we need a bigger house, we needed a bigger car! I could feel the resistance building up in my body as I battled with a loss of control.

Chris embraced me with his strong arms.

"We've got this. We're solid, and we know how to do this. We've both raised and cared for babies, even if it's been a while." He smiled at me wryly. "What I mean is, this isn't our first rodeo."

He was right. We'd had the past three years together to play and travel, blend our families, and strengthen our relationship. But with a new baby, will it all topple over? Again, I worried, *how will we keep our love on top?*

"We'll get help to juggle it all," Chris said, as if reading my thoughts. "Family, friends—we have a great support system to help us care for another child. And don't spirits tell you that our children choose their parents and their life experience? They have a sneak peek into what they're signing up for, right? This baby will adapt to our busy, full lives. We will still find time for us, I promise. Everything's going to be all right."

Everything's going to be all right. He was using Dad's line. I looked over at the clock—5:55. That's strange; it had to be nearly eight o'clock in the morning. Had Dad stopped the clock at 5:55? I squeezed Chris's hand tight as I recognized the signs and took in the meaning of the numbers—big changes are coming your way; release your fear, doubt, and worry and have faith it's all in divine time and the changes will be for the better.

GET IN THE FLOW

Day-to-day life can be unpredictable and messy, and can easily arouse feelings of overwhelm and anxiety. The trick is to not let ourselves get buffeted around too much by circumstances—the good and the not-so-good stuff—and instead allow ourselves to become part of the flow. I love this quote by Dr. Rob Gilbert: "It's all right to have butterflies in your stomach. Just get them to fly in formation."

So how do we quell the inner chaos?

Change your mind about it. The moment you start to panic, take a step back and pray for a shift in perspective. While we cannot control or change the circumstances, events, or people in our lives, we can change how we choose to see and feel about them.

A prayer I often use is: Dear God and guides, help me see through your eyes, hear with your ears, speak your words, and know as you know that divine perfection exists in all, and that all is right and well." Even when a situation feels far from "perfect," I pray for more trust and acceptance that my life is unfolding according to a perfect plan. I pray to get out of my resistance and fear and surrender to what I cannot see quite yet. I ask my guides and departed loved ones to shed more light on my life and help me gain a greater perspective.

Signs from the Other Side: LET GO, LET FLOW

I recall another reading with a woman who was struggling with fertility issues, along with fear and doubt.

"Your mom that died is here. Why is she flashing in my mind an image of you as a little girl sitting all alone in your room? She's making me feel scared and lonely."

"Mom died when I was only nine," Stacy said. "And Dad died two years later."

"So you were orphaned?"

"Yes," Stacy nodded.

"Do you have children?" I asked.

Stacy shook her head and started to cry. "My husband and I tried for years after I got married to get pregnant, and I never did."

"I think that Mom is bringing up this old feeling of abandonment and tying it to your pregnancy." I paused as her mother's spirit downloaded me with more feelings and messages. "Are you afraid *you* might die?" I asked on a hunch. "I'm picking up on a lot of fear and resistance around you getting pregnant."

Stacy looked at me as if she'd just found the missing piece to a puzzle. "Maybe unconsciously I've worried that if I had a baby, something might happen to me."

"You're afraid that if you become a mother," I suggested further, "that you will somehow abandon your child similar to how you felt left behind."

"I guess that is true."

"Mom is saying she's sorry she left you so young. But that same story is not going to play out with you and your children. Mom is moving her hands above your heart, as if she's lifting the fear away. She's also showing me a mental movie of you holding a newborn baby. My interpretation is that if you can release some of your resistance to getting pregnant, you'll have no problem conceiving. This is how powerful the mind-body connection is, and Mom is going to send you yellow butterflies to give you the courage you need to move past your fear."

"That's funny you should say that. I've always associated yellow butterflies with Mom."

"That's why she's bringing them up. Look for them."

A day later, Stacy sent me this e-mail: "While I was in the reading with you, my husband was visiting a job site (he's an architect) and said he was bombarded with YELLOW butterflies! His coworker even mentioned one that wouldn't stop swarming around his face. I know now it was Mom."

A constant reminder I receive from the departed and my guides is that the unseen forces are constantly at work, pushing and pulling us in different directions according to a bigger plan that's not always clear to us (and often it's ambiguous at best!). Through trust and faith, and by moving out of our own way, our lives will divinely unfold. When we can let go of our tendency or desire to control and set the intention each day to surrender, our lives will naturally flow in the direction they are meant to go.

How I Use This in My Life: **SHIFT FROM RESISTANCE INTO THE FLOW**

How do you know if you're in the flow?

Take a look at your life. Is your life flowing in a direction that feels right and on purpose? Do you generally feel content, grounded, and inspired? Are "miracles" and synchronicities daily occurrences in your life? In other words, do you often receive what you clearly ask for? Do positive relationships and opportunities tend to fall directly into your lap? Are you able to create and manifest, both personally and professionally, what you most desire with relative ease? If you answered yes to any of these questions, then take that as a sign that you are in the flow. Spirit is conspiring with you.

If your answer is no, then this is your sign that you're likely in a state of resistance—forcing, fighting, trying to control or manipulate outcomes, circumstances, and people in your life to give you what you want and need. To get out of resistance and into the flow, you simply need to ease up on your fear and doubt and set an intention to surrender to the unseen plan unfolding, and trust that it will become clear in time.

Ask your departed loved ones and guides: "Help me get out of my controlling head. Help me surrender my resistance and accept what is. Restore my faith in the bigger plan coming together behind the scenes. My life will flow and deliver to me exactly what I need if I allow it."

Signs from the Other Side: **TRUST THE UNKNOWN**

My brother Baruch is a perfect example of someone who surrendered his resistance to live a life that was "meant to be."

He'd reached the peak of his career as a synagogue rabbi, leading one of the most innovative and flourishing synagogues in the country. He was also compensated well for his work, earning more money than most of his colleagues and doing well by most anyone's standards. He and his family lived in a beautiful home in New England, and he'd become a pillar of his community.

What could be wrong with this picture?

Baruch woke up one morning with the title of one of Rabbi Harold Kushner's bestselling books—*When All You've Ever Wanted Isn't Enough*—ringing in his ears. Baruch thought, "I have everything I thought I wanted, but it's not enough. I love my wife. I love my kids. I love my friends and community. But I no longer love my job." Baruch realized that he now had a big decision before him. He'd just been asked to renew his contract with the synagogue—and it was a good one, which would likely ensure his professional, financial, and personal security and comfort for the rest of his life.

He said to me at the time, "My head has given me a thousand reasons why I must sign that contract, stay put, and make this work. But," he confided, "I no longer feel called, and I feel trapped."

So what did he do? He surrendered his resistance and listened to his heart—and it told him to move to the place that did call him: Israel. Yet, there was a small problem with this plan. It was 2014 and Israel was in the midst of war. Tourism was altogether absent, and the FAA had shut down most flights to Israel. It wasn't a good time to move to this particular country.

Just as Baruch was about to give up on his dream and renew his contract with the synagogue, out of the blue, he was invited by a friend on a solidarity trip to visit wounded civilians and soldiers near the Gaza Strip. He said that even with family and friends begging him not to go on this dangerous mission, it was the first time in years he felt truly guided. He recounted later, "I never felt more alive, more secure, and more at home. Literally, as missiles were being shot down overhead and after having been evacuated to a bomb shelter, I knew then and there that this was where me, my wife, and my children were meant to be.

It wasn't rational. It wasn't even sane. But it felt like this was the direction my life was meant to go."

Within the year, Baruch moved his family from New England to Israel, where he currently works full time as a grief counselor. I speak with him often, and while he admits that living in a foreign country is not easy or always comfortable, he has found relief away from a lifestyle that no longer "fit" and where now his days feel like they divinely flow.

AFTER CHRIS LEFT to drive the kids to school, I sat down in front of my altar and prayed: "God, guides, and departed loved ones, help me to stay out of my fearful mind in the months of big changes to come. I surrender, and I ask for your favor." I held out my hands and imagined my Team Spirit taking my worries and concerns from me. "Shift me into a state of appreciation and awe and acceptance of what is. Restore my faith in the unknown, and show me a clear sign that you're hearing me."

With my eyes still closed, I felt my "team" surround me. Their collective loving presence washed over me and held me. I clairsentiently felt them press in on my upper shoulders and back. And then, just as I'd asked, they showed me a sign—a glowing ring.

How I Use This in My Life: SHIFT FROM FREAK-OUT TO FLOW-TASTIC

From the outside, my life may seem divine and flow-tastic, but behind closed doors I'm learning the same lessons and dealing with the same challenges as anyone else. To help me shift out of a place of fear and toward faith that the earthly details will resolve themselves in divine time, I do a combination of the following:

Journal. Write down all of your most vulnerable, honest, and messy thoughts and feelings. Writing is a process of release, and you may discover that by simply writing down what's inside your head, some of the tension, apprehension, and fear you're holding in your mind and body are eased significantly. The process may also help you clarify how you're feeling and why. I love this quote by Barbara Rose, PhD, an expert in personal transformation: "Write down every conceivable reason that this situation can contribute towards your growth. Write down every way this experience can possibly set the stage for serving to uplift others. When you are complete, and have come to the other side of this experience, you will then know 'why' it happened."

Pray out loud. Ask for what you need or to help you make sense of what isn't clear. I often say the following prayer: "God, I give this to you. Help me. What is it I'm supposed to do, to know? I ask for your favor. Help to shift me out of a place of fear and back to faith."

Meditate. Ask your guides for their love and support and to provide you with clear direction forward. I will often ask: "Guides and departed loved ones, remind me, show me that there is a divine path forward for my life even though I can't fully appreciate or see it now." Be open to the signs, both subtle and literal, that you receive in meditation to validate or veto the path you're currently on.

Later that afternoon, as I drove to pick up Sam at his lacrosse practice, I wondered aloud, "Can I truly let go of my original plan of how I thought this next year of my life was going to play out? Can I truly surrender and relax with great ease into the unknown?" as author Tosha Silver writes in *Embrace the Divine.* In other words, can I walk my talk, and trust that I will receive what I need?

As I felt my fear creep up and catch in my throat, a car drove past me with the license plate GODSFVR. I did a double take. In prayer, I'd specifically asked for God's favor. Here was my sign!

But in case I missed it, my guides sent me another.

Later that same evening, during dinner prep, I ran down to the basement to our overflow fridge to get a gallon of milk. When I hit the bottom step, I noticed something lying in the middle of the floor. Where typically our basement is an organized mess, I had just cleaned it. I bent down to pick up the object in front of me—*a ring*. And not just any ole ring but an actual glowing ring of light! I recognized it immediately. On our first trip to Santa Barbara, Chris and I had serendipitously found a kid's jelly ring in the hotel garden. It lit up in a rainbow of colors, and we both remarked on the symbolism. It's a continuous ring of light," we said, "like the one that flows within us and between us." We brought it home, and it sat on Chris's meditation altar for nearly three years (long after the battery that lit it up died), until one day it mysteriously disappeared. We'd asked the kids if anyone had moved it, and none of them knew what ring we were talking about. And now, here I was, standing in the basement, and the ring was right at my feet, flashing its vibrant colors again. *How in the world? This thing hasn't worked in three years.*

I walked back upstairs holding the ring in my hand. "Where'd you find that?" Chris asked in amazement.

When I shared with him the whole story—my prayer and meditation, the license plate on the way home, and now this, he asked me to follow him into the entryway. "When I unlocked the front door tonight," Chris said, "I heard something fall and crash to the ground. It was one of your favorite plaques— the one that says FAITH."

This was my final validation that my guides had answered my prayers. The message, which applies to me just as it does to you, dear reader: Keep the faith. You are not alone. You are surrounded, protected, held, and loved from beyond. *Every day.* Your departed loved ones and guides hear you and your prayers for help and clarity. Surrender your fear, fight, resistance, and desire for control and you will receive God's favor. You will receive exactly what you need when you need it.

In the meantime, chill. Surrender. Trust. And let your life divinely unfold.

LIFE IS BEAUTIFUL: H(E)AVEN IS WITHIN

Chris proposed to me in the middle of the night in late 2014. His experience is that the truth comes out when our guard is down, so he woke me up out of a dead sleep and popped the question, "Will you marry me?" Chris maintains that once he's clear on something, he's all in and doesn't want to wait. We share that in common so my immediate response was "Yes!" He slipped a beautiful eternity band on my finger, and we held each other in the darkness, laughing and crying until we fell back asleep. We tentatively set a wedding date for over a year later on May 21, 2016. We were in no rush.

The truth was that as soon as we were engaged, we considered ourselves married in our hearts. Our engagement was our vow, and we both wore wedding rings soon after he proposed and referred to ourselves as married when meeting people and making dinner reservations. But we still wanted to make it official and looked forward to throwing a big wedding party for family and friends. We sent out general save-the-date cards, explaining to those invited that we'd send further details later. When my mom asked why we were waiting a year and a half to have a ceremony, the answer I gave her was, "What's the hurry? It's not like we're having more kids."

Well, when the next fall we found out I was pregnant and that the due date was May 21, 2016, our jaws dropped. I understood now why we'd arbitrarily saved this date—not for the wedding; we were unconsciously saving the date for this baby! Again, God had a plan all along.

A month before she was due to arrive, I sent out a group text to about sixty friends and family members, asking for *their* guesses for our baby's birth date. While I truly believe we're all born into this world when the stars align just right—astrologically and spiritually speaking (and I would honor whatever day the Universe had chosen for my baby to make her big debut)—I was still anxious as I waited for her and thought this would be a fun game to play. The responses I got back ranged from May 5 to May 27. I sensed it would be on or around the full moon, which I was tickled to discover was May 21!

On the morning of the 19th, I went into labor and headed to the hospital at 7:30 a.m. My contractions were five minutes apart, and I was in moderate, but not unbearable, pain. When I got into my room, I was told that the doctor on rotation that day was Dr. Levy, the same doctor who had delivered Sam. I was so happy to see him: Someone I knew and was comfortable with would be delivering my baby girl. "But," he apologized, "I have a mandatory doctor's meeting starting at noon. If we're going to deliver this baby, we only have three hours."

At nine o'clock, I was dilated to five centimeters. At eleven o'clock, I was at nine. Dr. Levy returned to my room and said, "I really want to deliver this baby. Let's all focus on you getting to ten centimeters in the next hour so you can start pushing."

My body was telling me it was unlikely, but I told him I'd try. As we sat together chatting about nothing in particular, the conversation turned to Omaha, where I grew up and where Dr. Levy said his late wife was from.

"She went to Central High School," he said. "Do you know of it?"

"Of course, that's where my dad went to school." I smiled.

"I love Omaha," he said. "One of my favorite pizza places is there—La Casa Pizzaria."

I laughed out loud. "My dad's all-time favorite pizza is from La Casa, and every time I visit home, I pick up a hamburger and Romano pie in honor of him."

As we continued to chat, I realized how much he reminded me of Dad. Why hadn't I noticed it before? Just as I thought this, the song changed on my Pandora channel to "How to Save a Life" by the Fray. This is Dad's song, and whenever I hear it, I know Dad is near. My eyes drifted to the corner of the room right behind Dr. Levy, where I could strongly sense his presence. "Hi, Dad," I thought to myself. "Thanks for showing up."

"Wow, you just did it," Dr. Levy exclaimed. "You're at ten centimeters. Are you ready to start pushing?"

"I'm ready." I was surrounded by my living and departed loved ones. I had all the support I needed.

Where Sam took over two hours to push out, and with excruciating pain, I delivered my baby girl in twenty minutes. I could psychically feel her little soul traveling down the tunnel to this world, as I recalled my dream from a few nights before. Wayne Dyer, who has served as one of my most inspirational spiritual teachers and who died recently, came to me in my dream. He was holding my naked baby, which I understood to mean "the naked Truth." He said, "Look into her eyes. She is a very special soul." Of course all babies are special, but as I remembered this dream in the midst of delivering, I was overcome with a sense of excitement and joy that I'd soon meet her.

Not a minute later, she dropped out of my body. As soon as Dr. Levy placed her on my chest and I looked into her eyes, I experienced a powerful déjà vu, the sense that this moment had happened before. I was familiar with this perfect, wonderful little creature. She and I—we'd stared at each other many times—in dreams and meditations and possibly in other lifetimes. In that moment of intense flashback, I had the clear knowing, like a soul remembering, that this pregnancy and birth was meant to be.

Over the years, I've heard Spirit reveal the same message countless times: Before being born, we have loosely scripted certain events and life lessons to show up along our path to serve as opportunities for us to learn and grow. When we bypass or resist these events, or somehow prevent them from happening, the Universe and our guides will continue to create new opportunities for them to manifest. Where I thought I was done having babies, this little girl found a way. A very unlikely and miraculous way, but she found it nonetheless. She fought especially hard to get in, and I will never again say never.

How well our lives divinely flow depends on our level of resistance. I understand now that our job as humans is to simply stick to our intention to show up every day in our highest selves and do our own unique version of purposeful work—and then let go of our grip on control and embrace the endless, unexpected blessings and miracles the Universe delivers.

"Let's call the actual birth time," Dr. Levy said to the nurse.

"Twelve forty," she said.

"Twelve forty?" I whispered. "As in 12-4?" I teared up and looked at Chris. This is the date that brought us together, when the Laughing Buddha handed me a rock and a strand of mala beads in meditation and told me that I was not alone—I was divinely guided, protected, and loved; the date when Chris showed up to Kabbalah class and offered to be my protector; 12-4, the date my life took a divine turn toward a brand new beginning.

And if that wasn't enough symbolism, I was discharged from the hospital on May 21, our original wedding date! This little one had outsmarted us all, arriving according to God's divinely timed schedule, ready or not.

WHAT'S IN A NAME?

During my pregnancy, both Chris and I had dreams where a spirit who announced herself as both Hasheena and Sha-henna visited us. We both intuitively knew that this spirit was our baby girl. Just as the spirits of our departed loved ones hear our prayers and can visit us in our dreams, so too can the spirits of our unborn children, whether in the womb or still on the Other Side. After these vivid dreams, we debated what to name her. We liked the idea of somehow honoring the names in the dreams, and also adding to the already established theme of "H" names in the family—Hannah, Harper, and Hadley. We finally stumbled upon the name "Haven" and both loved it instantly because it sounds so much like heaven. It turns out that heaven and haven have a similar meaning—both are places of loving shelter, which is exactly what I hope to provide her in this lifetime.

Funny; she's already doing the same for us.

As soon as Haven entered this life, I felt her presence pull our blended family together even closer. I soon realized, she's the anchor that will hold us all in place—wherever we are. While I do eventually want to move to a bigger house, I'm in less of a rush. We have our safe haven. We're already there.

As I held a sleeping Haven in my arms our first night home, I closed my eyes and counted my many blessings for another beautiful day in a body and thought about a quote from Denis Waitley: "Happiness cannot be traveled to, owned, earned, or worn. It is the spiritual experience of living every minute with love, grace, and gratitude." And I would add to that: It is enhanced by the knowing that divine guidance, assistance, and abundance are always within and around us.

I looked down at Haven, my physical manifestation of abundance, and thought about my wishes for her. "Just be you," I whispered to her. "I am here to hold space for you to fulfill whatever it is that you've come here to do." I kissed her on the top of her head.

And then, I began to sing. Very low and slow, I sang one of my favorite lullabies, "Golden Slumbers" by the Beatles. I flashed back to my own childhood when I was discouraged from singing. "You're no good," my brother often teased. "You're off-tune," Dad would chime in. As I whispered the sweet words, "Sleep pretty darling, do not cry and I will sing a lullaby," I recognized that Haven and I were already helping to heal one another. *I will always encourage you to speak your truth, and you are my messenger to remind me that it is safe to use my voice.*

While I've mastered my ability to hear and give voice to the dead, I spent too much of my life not speaking up, not putting words to and giving a voice to my intuitive knowing—my feelings that know what they know—as they've related to my own life. Well, here I sit, now ready to rewrite this story, to heal this childhood wound, not only for myself, but also for Haven. A pattern of silence, shrinking down and feeling powerless ends today and begins differently with her. I reclaim my voice. I reclaim my power. And together, we will sing.

We all have hurts—often childhood wounds—that we carry with us throughout our lives until we step forward with the courage and resolve to heal them. These wounds are sometimes unconscious, but we can bring them to the forefront of our minds for healing through mindfulness: by paying greater attention to the repeated situations, patterns, and dynamics within our relationships that trigger feelings of discomfort and hurt. Every time your wound is reopened becomes an opportunity for self-discovery, self-love, and healing.

As I drifted off to sleep with Haven snuggled in my arms, I felt the presence of my dad and my guides surround me as they flashed in my mind's eye a black and yellow butterfly, my sign for transformation and spiritual truth,

whether it's from life into death or an ending of one chapter and the beginning of another in the course of one's life. I clearly heard their words and
knew they weren't only for me, but for you, dear reader, as well:

> Stand up and breathe, wave your arms up high and allow your spirit
> to rise, to soar, and to reach up to God. Fill your body with its abun-
> dant love and light. Feel it trickle into every corner and crease of your
> being until your spirit begins to hum. Do you hear it? What does it
> say? Open your mouth and speak. Sound your trumpet loud. What is
> your truth? Whatever it is, it is yours and for that reason it must be
> spoken. Whether your words inspire or challenge others, have faith
> that you are on the right path and that along the way you are never
> alone. You are held, and you are loved. Be free and know your guides
> and departed loved ones sing a sweet tune to you, through you, and
> will carry you wherever you are and wherever you need to go next. It is
> safe to surrender your fear and receive God's favor—innumerable bless-
> ings, miracles, and true abundance are yours.

SIGNS FROM BEYOND

O ur departed loved ones and guides use a special "sign language" to let us know when they are around. Some of these universal signs will be applicable over your lifetime, while others may pertain only to a certain period in your life or to a particular departed loved one or guide.

Setting the intention to be open to the signs is your best strategy for noticing them. While they may feel small and easy to dismiss at first, signs from the Other Side often increase in frequency and size when they are focused on, acknowledged, and continually requested.

There are endless numbers of signs (for a more extensive list, see my book *Spirited*). Following is a list of the top fifteen that spirits use to validate or answer a question you may have asked or to simply remind you that you are guided from beyond and never alone.

Angel bumps: Spirits often reach out to you very subtly and impress you with a sense of love by brushing your arm or neck or by gently placing their hands on your back or shoulders. This is often referred to as getting the chills, or angel bumps. If you sense a presence in the room with you, sitting next to you, or watching over you, consider this a sign that a loving spirit is answering your call for help, guidance or support.

Animals: Similar to children, animals easily pick up on the departed because they're highly sensitive creatures. When your pets look like they're watching an invisible fly move around the room; when they whimper or growl in a certain direction but at nothing in particular; when they act as if they're playing with someone, running in circles, jumping all over the place, or swatting the air—they may be recognizing spirits. Sure, a lot of times animals just behave this way. But when unusual behavior is accompanied by a request for spiritual intervention, it's very possible your departed loved ones or guides have answered your call.

Children: Have you ever noticed that kids can say the most insightful things—wise beyond their years—at just the right time? Young children often serve as little messengers for our departed loved ones and spirit guides. The departed connect easily with children because they live in the present moment and are much more dialed in to their intuitive senses. They feel and sense the presence of Spirit and will relay messages from beyond without judgment or question.

Coins: Spirit can inspire coins to appear in random and unusual places as a way to get our attention—often as a message of prosperity or to encourage you to value your worth. Because coins, especially pennies, are often found lying around in the home, at the bottom of your purse, or in the subway or train station, it may be hard to distinguish between spiritual intervention and chance circumstance. So when you find coins, pay attention to patterns that consistently reappear. Do you typically find dimes? Do you often find a penny and a nickel together? Does the date on the coin hold any meaning for you? Have you asked for financial help from your guides? The words "In God We Trust" can be a reminder to have faith and trust that abundance is your birthright.

Dreams: Spirits like to communicate with us in this altered mental state because our thinking mind is turned down and our intuitive knowing is turned up. When we're visited by the departed and our guides in our dreams, we're often left with lasting impressions and insights that help direct us forward in our waking life.

Electricity (lights, electronics, technology, appliances): It's easy for spirits to manipulate electricity and cross wires, so to speak, because both spirits and electricity are forms of energy that vibrate at a high frequency and are highly charged. Look for lights flickering in the house, lightbulbs blowing out, or disturbance with television sets, radios, appliances, and computers. These are all typical spirit moves, and often just their way of saying hello.

Feathers: Feathers are often a beautiful sign that your departed loved ones, guides, and angels are near, loving, and supporting you from beyond. When you find or notice white feathers in unusual places, consider this a sign from your guardian angel.

Formations in the sky: Rainbows are my personal "sign" for the Other Side and they are a common symbol of divine love. If you ask your departed loved ones or guides for assistance and a rainbow appears shortly after that, know your prayers have been heard and are being answered. A rainbow serves as a good reminder that you are connected to divine love within you, as you, and that you're never alone.

Music: Your departed loved ones and guides may communicate with you through a song title or lyric that reminds you of them at the exact time you are thinking about them. They may also try and provide you with clarity and guidance through a series of songs with a resounding theme or message that answers a question you have about a particular situation.

Numbers: Do you have a favorite number or number sequence? Spirit will often use number patterns that hold meaning for you to attempt contact. Be on the lookout (but don't look for) repetitive number sequences that hold special meaning to you or a departed loved one, such as birth dates, death dates, anniversary dates, or "lucky" numbers. I've built a whole sign language of numbers with my guides and by using Doreen Virtue's book *Angel Numbers 101* as a reference guide. Every day, I notice number signs and sequences via license plates, vanity tags, page numbers, street addresses, receipt totals, and time stamps.

Scents: Have you ever noticed a strong odor or fragrance in the air around you, with no indication of where it was coming from? This could be your departed loved ones manifesting a specific scent that you associated with them in life, to let you know they are still with you. It might be a perfume, cologne, cigarette odor, the smell of certain foods, or any other distinguishable and unique scent.

Signs: Sometimes the departed and your guides will use literal signs to capture your attention. These "signs"—billboards, advertisements, street names, shop signs, and flyers—generally address a specific question you want an answer to. Signage is everywhere, so it's up to you to discern the difference between messages that are inspired or insignificant. This is one of the instances where you really need to trust that you will know it when you see it.

Sparks or flashes of light: Spirits are energetic beings of light, and they sometimes appear in photographs and to our plain eye as orbs, shimmers and flashes of light. When I see a spark of light appear to the side or above my client, I know that I'm communicating with his or her spirit guide, and the brighter the light, the older and more highly evolved and enlightened the spirit is.

Synchronicities: When you experience a series of "coincidences" or synchronicities, it means you are on the right track and being divinely guided and supported.

Wings: Spirits love to manipulate winged creatures such as butterflies, birds, hummingbirds, dragonflies, ladybugs, flies, and bees. Spirits will inspire these creatures to fly in our direction and land on us to get our attention. Before swatting them away, consider that they are messengers from beyond.

SPIRITUAL TOOLS

We all have the ability to connect with our higher guidance, be it our Team Spirit or our own intuitive knowing. In fact, no one is more tuned in to your departed loved ones and guides than YOU! That said, sometimes we need a little extra validation or clarity.

Candles: I liken the flame of a candle with the spiritual light within each of us that energetically connects us with the higher energies of the unseen world and with everyone around us in the physical world. You can use this spiritual tool in the following ways:

> **Connect with Spirit:** Spirits often encourage me to light candles to draw them in, as the high vibrational frequency of the flame is easily recognized by them. Light attracts light, as like attracts like, which is why I make a habit of lighting a candle before I do any type of reading. As I light the wick, I invite in loving spirits with clear messages from the Other Side.

> **Manifesting:** In addition to using candles to invite connectivity with spirits, you can also use candles to manifest a desired outcome. This practice is referred to as "candle magic" or "candle burning." The basic principles are to visualize what you most want to manifest in your life and then project that visualization on the burning flame. This can be done with eyes open or closed; maintaining focus on the flame with your desired outcome in mind is what's important. Candle burning can be used for protection, overcoming bad habits, attracting people or personal objects into your life, repairing health, and developing a stronger connection to your departed loved ones.

> **Meditation:** I almost always start my meditations by lighting a candle and offering a prayer of gratitude for the presence of Spirit to protect me. I then meditate on the flame for a few minutes,

setting the intention to draw the candlelight into my body and ignite my own internal spark. I visualize this light growing and expanding within me, filling me with love and light. As I go deeper into my meditation, I invite intuitive guidance and messages from beyond into my consciousness.

Crystals: I like to place crystals—especially clear quartz—on my altar or throughout my house and office. It was once only an intuitive belief that clear quartz held psychic and healing powers, but modern measuring equipment has since proved the belief to be correct (I'm not sure how, but they did!). Quartz is called the master stone, because it can do so much, including: clear your energetic space externally and internally; reduce stress and help to balance and calm you; and strengthen your clairvoyance. In order to soak up the benefits of quartz crystal, simply position it where you spend much of your time, such as your bedroom, office, or an altar. You can also wear it in a piece of jewelry or carry it in your pocket. It's important to note, that as with any spiritual tool, a crystal is not a magic tool. Meaning, it does not work solely on its own, but heightens and strengthens your own intuitive power and connectivity to Spirit.

Divinity cards: Angel, tarot, affirmation, or divination card readings can be incredibly helpful, and amazingly accurate, when you desire a clear read on a situation or to answer a question you may have for yourself or a loved one. Decks can be purchased at most bookshops, new age and spiritual shops, and online. Amazon is a good place to start, with a simple search for "angel cards" or "affirmation cards." Choose the deck that you feel intuitively drawn to. There is no "right" one for anyone. I have several decks that I've collected over the years, and I refer to them quite often, sometimes asking for guidance around a specific question I have or to help me set an intention for my day. To watch a video on how I conduct an angel card reading on myself, visit Rebecca's Inner Circle on rebeccarosen.com.

Essential oils: Essential oils are essences derived from various plants. They can be used to beautify and purify your environment, as well as to raise your energetic vibration; and enhance your psychic experiences. There are many ways to use essential oils. Put them in your bath, rub them on candles, use them in a diffuser, spray them in the air, or anoint yourself with them. Essential oils have become a regular part of my everyday routine. A few of my favorites and their uses include:

Lavender: integrating, balancing, healing, protecting, purifying; opens third-eye chakra

Rose: cleansing, healing, balancing, protective; opens heart chakra

Rosemary: protective, cleansing, psychic stimulant; dispels negativity; opens heart chakra and third-eye chakra

As with anything, there's not a one-size-fits-all when it comes to oils, so follow your nose and trust your higher guidance. If you're drawn to a specific scent, or if a name on a bottle stands out to you, trust that it's calling you for a reason.

Intention boards: I have a tradition where at the start of any new phase, like a new year or major transition in my life, I create an intention board. I sit down with a stack of magazines and I cut out pictures, phrases, and words that capture the feeling and intention of the physical objects, experiences, and feelings I want to manifest during the new phase. At different times, I've desired to travel more, learn a new skill or talent, advance my career, and be the best mother, wife, employer, and friend I can be.

I then paste these words and images down on a poster board and hang it in my meditation space, where I can reflect on it daily. It serves as a collage of my hopes, dreams, and goals that I intend to bring into my physical experience in the near future. If the idea of posting your goals and intimate dreams down on paper scares you, challenge yourself to be brave and ask for what you want. That's the first step to manifesting it! In addition to, or as an alternative to, creating a vision board, consider other ways to be inspired day-to-day. Throughout my home and office, I have coffee mugs, candles, and artwork with positive affirmations that serve to remind me of my biggest dreams and deepest intentions.

Mala beads: Malas, or Buddhist prayer beads, are a traditional tool used to count the number of times a mantra or prayer is recited while meditating. Malas are typically made with 18, 27, 54, or 108 beads. In Tibetan Buddhism, malas of 108 beads are used, and these are the ones I prefer. For the past several years, I have started and ended my day with these special beads. In the morning, I wrap them on as I recite a short prayer and set my intention for the day, and at the end of the day I unwrap them with a prayer of gratitude to Spirit and my guides for another beautiful day in a body. Mala beads can be purchased at any Tibetan gift shop, where employees should be able to help you find a set of beads that is best suited for your intention. I have several strands that I'm drawn to on different days for different reasons. While malas were originally intended for meditation, they can also be worn as a physical reminder to remain present and aware of our daily prayers and intentions and of our connection to the Other Side.

Smudge spray: There are many ways to clear the negative, outside energy around you, and one of my favorite practices is the Native American ritual of smudging. Traditional smudging involves burning sage leaves, which create a powerful smoke in the air. But burning this strong-smelling herb isn't always practical or allowed. (While it's a weekly ritual in my own home, it's completely off limits for me to do in my shared office building.)

At work then, I typically clear the air with a smudge spray. There are several great brands available that combine essential oils, sea salts, and other herbs such as sage. I love my Smudge in Spray, which is a blend of medical-grade essential oils, holy waters from around the world, sacred site essences, and Bach flower essences. Shift the mood and energy of your living and personal space with essential oils like neroli to alleviate anxiety and neutralize negative energy; sandalwood and sage for protection; and orange and lemon to cleanse and uplift. As you spray your office or living space, set the intention to clear away any toxic or sticky energy that you or the space around you has absorbed.

You might also ask your spirit guides to pitch in by helping to remove any and all darkness, negativity, and fear from your external environment. There are many scents available, so simply select one that smells good to you and naturally lifts your spirit.

ACKNOWLEDGMENTS

Once again, I am in complete awe at the divine orchestration behind the creation of this book and the many miracles that followed. Where I set out to write one book, as fate would have it, the Universe had other plans! As the saying goes, man plans and God laughs! Shortly into the process, this book took a turn in a different direction, one I never imagined possible.

Just as in my work doing readings as a spiritual medium, I surrendered to God's plan, showing up as the willing vessel and then simply getting out of the way, trusting Spirit to guide both the content and the process in which it would unfold. It is with great honor and pride that I get to share this extraordinary journey with so many fellow seekers, spiritual companions, and friends. Most importantly, I'm eternally grateful for the continued presence of my Team Spirit, both in heaven and on earth.

I am blessed to call Samantha Rose my beloved cowriter and cherished friend. It's clear we were predestined to put our heads and hearts together, to collaborate and create what is now our third divinely inspired book. It is because of her invaluable writing skills, compassion for my experiences, and appreciation of the work that this book was born, yet again taking on a life of its own!

My rock star literary agent and dear friend, Yfat Reiss Gendell, continues to be one of my greatest pillars of support for both me and my work. My books exist as a result of her desire and ongoing dedication for nearly the past decade to help me create a platform to teach, share, and inspire the world with my message. While I don't believe in luck, I truly feel lucky and blessed to work with her and the entire Foundry team. A special thanks to the following at Foundry Literary + Media, whose ongoing hard work and support have helped me every step of the way: Editorial Assistant Jessica Felleman, Foreign Rights Director Kirsten Neuhaus, Foreign Rights Associate Heidi Gall, prior Foreign Rights Associate Jessica Regel, Film Entertainment Director Richie

Kern, Controller Sara DeNobrega, and Finance Team Associate Alex Rice.

While the content in this book was divinely inspired, it is because of my fabulous editor, Leah Miller, and her unwavering confidence and faith in me that I was able to bring forth an authentic account of the miracles and wisdom from Spirit. Leah provided me with her support, both as a seasoned editor and as a cheerleader in getting behind my message, finding the highest and best way for me to share this wisdom with the world. I am grateful for our new partnership and friendship!

And a special thank-you, too, to the wonderful team at Rodale— Publisher Gail Gonzales, Editorial Director Jennifer Levesque, Editorial Assistant Anna Cooperberg, Executive Director of Strategic Development Yelena Nesbit, Assistant Manager of Communications Susan Turner, Sub Rights Director Rhea Lyons, Senior Marketing Manager Angie Giammarino, Suzee Skwiot and the Rodale Wellness Team, Senior Project Editor Hope Clarke, Associate Art Director Christina Gaugler, and the Macmillan sales force. I thank you all for welcoming me into your "home," full of enthusiasm, support, and faith in the evolution of this book. The Rodale team has been a breath of fresh air to work with, and I am truly appreciative of their ongoing dedication in doing their part to ensure this book ends up in the hands of the countless like-minded spiritual seekers in need.

I have always been a team player, and without a few key people there is no way I could effectively reach my audience and sustain the level of quality and care that we pour into every area of my business. I am humbled to have the ongoing support and love of my office staff: my rock star COO Jacqueline Sene, my earth angel assistant Elizabeth Buckius, the super savvy marketing expertise of Sara Quigley, social media support of Danny Schiff, and the tech savvy media assistance of Kwame Johnson. It has been an honor to collaborate with my brother Rabbi Baruch HaLevi, in creating materials and offerings to serve the countless spiritual warriors and spark seekers out there to live their best lives.

I'm also beyond thrilled to have the assistance of the entire team at Peaceful Media, who have helped me broaden my reach in both my audience and the content produced to serve the growing number of people desiring and in need of my spiritual tools and teachings.

To my family:

My husband, Chris, who has given me the ultimate gift of knowing love in its highest expression as my twin flame. He lives by his motto, "Don't let the extraordinary become ordinary just because it's common," and he demonstrates his awareness and appreciation of both *me and my gift* every day as he makes what's important to me important to him. His relentless example of integrity, commitment, perseverance, and strength has served as my inspiration and compass as we both continue to show up and do God's work, while keeping our love on top.

To my children, Jakob, Sam, and Haven, for whom I am deeply honored to have brought into this world, and my bonus (step) children, Hannah, Harper, and Hadley, recognizing each of these individual expressions of love and light as my greatest teachers and soul mates. I am so appreciative of the ease and grace in which our blended family came to be, and the rich, juicy experience it continues to be as we grow together.

To my beloved mom, who always hoped and dreamed I would one day have a daughter, to know the joy a mother-daughter relationship brings just as our own. And it is because of her example of unconditional love and care that I am able to pay it forward to my own. She has taken care of me on every level these past few years, proving there is no greater love than a mother's love for her child, along with the love and support of my stepdad, Howard, something I will always remember and appreciate!

To my brothers, Baruch and Zach—from the time I was young, B, as he's known, has been my mentor, role model, and one of my closest soul companions. His courage, faith, and drive to live an authentic life and to be of service in the healing and empowerment of others has been hugely inspirational to me. Our work together the past couple of years has been both an honor and a privilege to share, learning and growing together as we work to redeem our father's legacy in staying the course and keeping the faith as we journey through life's ups and downs. I feel incredibly blessed and grateful to B for being this guiding light for me, for all.

Zach defines what it means to be true to yourself and follow your bliss. His strong work ethic and commitment to keeping it real and simple have been refreshing to witness, and I am thankful for his presence as my reminder to do the same.

My sister-in-law Ariela, who's been the poster child for what it means to be a fabulous mother, putting her family first and in keeping true to a balanced, meaningful, and purposeful life.

Grandma Flo, who passed at age 95 and embodied what it meant to be a living expression of joy and appreciation, an example I only hope to live up to! Her positive attitude and belief in me have served to help me be who I am today.

To my soul sisters:

Ariel, who has served as my energy healer for over 10 years, keeping me grounded and real, while filling me with the light and love of God and my angels, allowing me to soar both as a spiritual medium and as a human being. I value and cherish our time together, forever grateful that she walked into my life 10 years ago as a response to my prayer for healing.

Katie, Rebecca, and Laura, a few of my oldest and closest friends and soul sisters: I am blessed to have these special ladies by my side as we move through this messy, wild ride of life!

Vanna, one of the kindest, humblest, and most loving souls I know, serving as my example of what it looks like to stay grounded and connected to our Truth, as she shines her light and love for the world to see and feel.

A few more earth angels: Diana, Carolyn, Paula, Stacy, Kimmie, Lanie, Janie, Aliza, Rachel, Kelley and Lo, along with some of my childhood besties, Jamie, Carin, Nikki, Shana, and Cari, who each love and accept me for who I am today. I am grateful for their continued support, both personally and professionally.

Elizabeth A, who has been an earth angel in our family's lives, caring for our family and household over the past 10 years. It takes a village, and she has truly been the glue, offering ongoing quality of care and help in every way! To the rest of my family, the many special friends, and spiritual companions who have blessed my life in little and big ways over the years, I am truly thankful for the richness and depth of connection and care they have shared with me.

My deepest thanks goes out to all my clients who shared their stories in this book, along with all the brave souls who have sat with me over the years, opening their hearts and minds to the experience of my work. I am blessed to have such a loyal clientele. And a special shout-out to all my Inner Circle members and friends, who have allowed me the ongoing opportunity to share my gift in meaningful ways. Each person who has crossed my path has done so for a reason, molding me into the spiritual and human being that I am.

My guides, MC and M3, and my Dad in spirit, whose guidance and spiritual presence have served as my strength, courage, and guiding light each step of the way. The endless miracles, signs, and blessings showered upon me are forever appreciated and gratefully welcomed!

To all of the above, deep and heartfelt thanks and all love, as I would not be where I am without you and your presence along my journey. Namaste.

INDEX

A

Abundance, 66–75
  law of, 70
Acceptance, mantra for self-love and, 45–46
Addictions, 64
Affirmations. *See also* Visualizations
  for abundance, 70–71, 74–75
  for cutting negative cords, 148
  for energetic cleansing, 83
  forgiveness, 148
  on gratitude for former friend, 103
  for mind and body, 51
  for releasing hurt and resentment, 107–8
  for spirit cleansing, 51–52
African safari, 67–68
Afterlife, 86, 126–27
Airport, encounter at, 170–71
Angel bumps, 187
Angels, as messengers, 120–21
Animals, 130, 187
Archangel Michael, 136, 138, 148
Ariel, 82–83
Art, 130
Ashes, dog's, 147
Audience readings, meditation and
        preparation before, 7
Automatic writing, 2

B

Baby girl, 1–2, 3–4, 6, 22
  birth of, 181–84
  first night with, 185–86
  naming, 184
  niece's birth and, 15–16
  spirit of, 164, 169
Babysitter, 59–62, 65–66, 78–79, 131
Back pain, 52–53
Balance, 33–34
  work-life, 22–29
Bankruptcy, 68–69
Baths, salt, 83
Bay, James, 152
Beads, mala, 193–94
Best friends, 93, 97–99
Billboards, 189

Blended family, 121–23, 184
Blue light, 136
Body, physical
  activities for powerful, 65
  freedom from obsession with, 45–46
  spirits' desire for, 44
  weight concerns, 37–38, 40, 43
Breath, in meditation, 9
Brian (first husband), 17–22, 101–2, 135–37
"Bridge, The," 146
Brown, Brené, 30
Buddha, Laughing, 136, 137, 138
Bumblebee sting, 11
Business, husband starting new, 75–77
Butterflies, 173, 174

C

Campbell, Ross, 116–17
Cancer, 117–18
Candles, 191–92
Cards
  divinity, 192
  playing, 149, 150
Cell phone, God dial on, 133
Chakras. *See* Throat center
Chapman, Gary, 116–17
Children
  acknowledging feelings of, 125–26
  being present with, 116
  connection-sparking practices for,
        129–31
  death and afterlife talk with, 126–27
  explaining heaven to, 128–29
  love languages of, 116–17
  meditation for, 126
  as messengers, 187–88
  music and, 129
  Other Side and, 127–28
  preparing and helping, 125–26
  projecting worry onto, 123
  raising five, 113–14
  readings for connection with, 130
  spirits of unborn, 184
  white light charge for, 115
  worry about divorce impact on, 123

Chris (husband), 32, 56–57, 155–57
  bankruptcy as gift to, 68–69
  blended family and, 121–23, 184
  as energetic match, 152–53
  Kabbalah class meeting with, 137–38
  protection role of, 137–38
  as soul mate, 138–39
  Target incident, 69–70
Clairaudience, 3
Claircognizance, 60
Clairsentience, 3
Clarity, 90, 179
Clearings, 56
Coins, 188
College education, 12–13
Community, connection creating, 88–89
Compassion, 30
Conflict, between head and heart, 60–62
Congratulations, from Amy's spirit fathers,
        118–19
Connection
  best friends telepathic, 98
  community created through, 88–89
  family circle for, 130
  to God, Spirit, 84–85, 191
  loss of, 155–57
  meditation on inner light and, 88
  prayer for, 85
  reasons for lack of, 5
  sparking child's, 129–31
  with spirit, 191
  suicide and, 86–87
  visualization for, 85
Cord, silver, 85
Cords
  affirmation for cutting negatively
        charged, 148
  cutting relationship, 145–46
Costco receipts, 60–61, 131, 132. See also
        Babysitter
Couples, visualization for, 141
Crystals, 192

D
Death
  guilt over son's, 40–44
  soul contract on time of, 41
  talking to children about, 126–27
Destiny, as daughter's name, 47
Diabetes, 46–47
Distraction, 90

Divine timing, 35, 104–5
Divinity cards, 192
Divorce, 17–22, 95–96, 123, 136
  prayers and guidance after, 135–37
Dog, ashes of ex-husband's, 147
Dreams, 12–13, 184
  as signs, 188
  spirit visitation differentiated from, 1
Dressing, energetic, 55–56
Drinking problem, 139–40
Drug overdose, 99–100
Dyer, Wayne W., 96, 183

E
Eating
  emotional, 44–45
  negative thinking while, 49–50
Electricity, 188
Emotional eating, 44–45
Emoto, Masaru, 49
Empathy, mediumship and, 53–55
Empowerment, 65–66
Energy, 28, 151
  cleansing external, 82–84
  dressing energetically, 55–56, 83
  energetic match in relationship, 151–52
  protection, 55–56
  recharging, 157–58
  shift from heavy to light, 50–52
Engagement, 181
Essential oils, 192–93
Exit point, 41

F
Faith, 172–73, 176, 179, 180
Families
  blended, 121–23, 184
  connection through family circles, 130
  as predestined, 123
Family reunions, readings involving, 38–40
  angelic messengers and, 120–21
  on cutting cords, 145–46
  on finances, 75–77
  introductions and, 4–6
  on inviting in new love, 149–50
  on love as priority, 154–55
  on practicing forgiveness, 147–48
  self-worth message during, 62–63
  on speaking truth, 143–44
  spirits of two fathers, 117–19
  on suicides, 86–87, 120–21

on unexpected life event, 170–72
on unhappy marriage, 143–44
Fathers, spirits of both, 117–19
Father-son patterns, 119–20
Feathers, 188
Feelings
  acknowledging children's, 125–26
  language of, 61
  meditation on, 126
  silencing, 142–43
  sitting with uncomfortable, 82
Fiddle, 170
Financial loss, from powerlessness, 62
Floating sensation, 40–41
Flow, 173–74, 176–79
Food, 51
  addiction to, 64
  self-medicating with, 47
Forgiveness, 147, 148, 149, 150
Formations in the sky, as messengers,
    188–89
Four Agreements, The (Ruiz), 106
Friends and friendships
  assessing, 109–10
  best, 93, 97, 98–99
  divine timing and, 104–5
  on fringe, 103–4
  gratitude for former, 103
  ground crew, 97–98, 109
  hurt from, 107–8
  knowing when to end, 105–7
  maintaining, 100–103
  making new, 110–11
  prayer on, 110
  psychic intuitive, 100–103
  shifting from loss to gratitude for, 103
  soul mates as, 98–99
  unhealthy, 108–9

G
Gilbert, Rob, 173
Giving, 69–70
God. See also Spirit
  connection with, 84–85, 191
  favor of, 179, 186
  feeling separate from, 85, 86
God dial, 133
Gossip, 95–96
Grandma Babe, 2–3, 94
Gratitude, 103, 161–62
Grief, 143

Ground crew, 97–98, 109
Grounding, with white light, 56

H
HaLevi, Baruch, 140, 150–51, 176–78
Happy Buddha, Chris as, 138
Haven (newborn daughter), 184–86
Hawks, 13–14
Hay, Louise, 45
Head-heart conflict, 60–62
Healing, responsibility and, 139–40, 141
Health, food and, 51
Heart, 60–62, 161
Heart attack, 3
Heaven, 128–30, 155
Hotei (Laughing Buddha), 136, 137
House, move to new, 26
How I Use This in My Life
  for abundance, 74–75
  for assessing friendships, 109–10
  for changing heaviness to lightness, 50–52
  for clarity, 90
  for clearing external energy, 82–84
  for community connection, 88–89
  encouraging children to feel, 126
  energetic dressing, 55–56
  for energy recharge, 157–58
  for flow, 176, 178–79
  following impulses to call soul mates, 98
  freedom from body obsession, 45–46
  for giving and receiving, 70–71
  for gratitude, 161–62
  lining up, 15
  love languages of children, 116–17
  for more light, 96–97
  practicing forgiveness, 148
  prayer for connection, 85
  resistance transformed into flow, 176
  self-worth, 64–66
  for shifting from loss to gratitude, 103
  sparking child's connection, 129–31
  for speaking up, 142–43
  striving for balance, 33–34
  for trust in divine timing of friendships,
      104–5
  visualization for freedom from hurts,
      107–8
  white light charge for children, 115
Husband, new business started by, 75–77.
    See also Brian (first husband); Chris
    (husband)

I

Immaculate Conception, 169
Imperfections, 30
Inner light, 88, 96
Intention board, 8
Intuition, trust in, 60–62, 125
Iowa Hawkeyes, 13–14
Irritable bowel syndrome, 143
Israel, 177–78

J

Jewelry, letting go of, 38–40
Journaling, 178–79
Judgments, inner light as diminished by, 96
Jung, C. G., 13

K

Kabbalah class, 137–38
Kushner, Harold, 177

L

Lane, Diane, 145
Languages
    children's five love, 116–17
    of Higher Self, 61
Last Goodbye, The, 46, 54, 170
Laughing Buddha (Hotei), 136, 137
Lavender oil, 193
Law of abundance, 70
"Let It Go," 152
Lexus SUV, 67
Life review, 39
Life's work, service as, 69
Light
    blue, 136
    from dim to, 96–97
    flashes of, 189–90
    meditation on inner, 88
    white, 15, 55–56, 115
Lining up, 6–8
Loss, shifting to gratitude from, 103
Lou Gehrig's disease, 42
Love
    as first priority, 153–55, 159
    inviting in new, 149–50
    visualizing children feeling, 117
Love languages, of children, 116–17

M

Mala beads, 193–94
Manifesting, 191
Mantras, 9, 40, 45–46, 70, 89, 193

Marriage, 140–41
    fear of ending, 171–72
    letting go of, 145–46, 149–50
    respectfully ending, 19
    soul mates, divorce and, 17–18
    speaking truth in unhappy, 143–44
Material objects, enjoyment from, 67
Mattress, new, 52–53
Medication overdose, 55
Meditation, 6. *See also* Affirmations; How I
        Use This in My Life; Visualizations
    altar, 7–8
    basic instructions for, 191–92
    breath and, 9
    for children, 126
    daily practice of, 9–10
    on inner light, 88
Mediumship, 50–55
    insecurity over, 94–95
Michael (archangel), 136, 138, 148
Mind, affirmation for body and, 51
Mindfulness, 89–91, 91–92
Miscarriage, 97, 163–64
Music, 129, 189
Myss, Caroline, 28

N

Nature, heaven and, 130
Neck pain, 53–54
Negativity, 46–50, 83, 148
New house, 26
Numbers, 167, 189
    birthday, 69–70
    cell phone God dial, 133
    connection validation through, 157
    repetitive sequences of, 26, 55
    on stopped clock, 173

O

Other Side. *See also* Signs, from Other
        Side; Spirits and spirit guides
    breaking through, 4
    morning time used by, 1–2
    talking to children about, 127–28
Overdose, 55, 99–100

P

Panic attacks, 20–21
Parents, soul contract on, 124
People-pleasing, 61
Perfection, letting go of, 33
Playing cards, 149, 150

Poppy, 149–50
Power
  giving away, 132
  stepping into, 65–66
  taking back, 96
Powerlessness
  financial loss from, 62
  visualization to address, 65
Prayer
  for clarity and faith, 179
  for connection with God, 85
  after divorce, 135–37
  on friendships, 110
Predestination, 123–25
  surprise pregnancy and, 169–70
Pregnancy, reading on fear as blocking,
    174–75
Pregnancy, surprise, 162–67, 168, 178
  birth date and labor, 181–84
  dream of names during, 184
  faith and, 172–73, 179–80
  predestination and, 169–70
Projecting, onto children, 123
Prosperity. See Abundance
Protection, 55–56, 81–84
  husband Chris's role of, 137–38

R
Readings. See also Family reunions,
    readings involving; specific topics
  clear and accurate, 50
  clearings before and after, 56
  connecting with children through, 130
  nausea during, 53–55
  phone, 52–56
  preparation before audience, 7
  small group, 30–32
  spirit line-up before, 30
Receipts, Costco, 60–61
Receiving, 69–70, 77–78
  financial abundance, 73–74
Relationships. See also Marriage
  asking for sign to stay in or leave, 144–45
  cutting cords of, 145–46
  ending, 144
  energetic match in, 151–52
  needs and, 158–59
  new patterns for, 119–20
  self-love as basis of, 150–51
  spirit guides on, 139
  two halves in, 140
  visualization for couples, 141

Resistance, 176
Resting place, afterlife, 86
Riches. See Abundance
Ringing in ears, 3
Rock, gift of, 136, 137
Rosemary oil, 193
Rose oil, 193
Roses, yellow, 118–19
Ruiz, Don Miguel, 106

S
Salt baths, 83
Scents, 189
Self-love, 150–51
  mantra for acceptance and, 45–46
Self-medicating, with food, 47
Self-worth, 62–69, 71–73
Signs, from Other Side
  about, 187
  on abundance and self-worth, 71–73
  angel bumps, 187
  animals, 187
  asking for, 11–12
  billboards, street signs, 189
  butterflies, 174
  children, 187–88
  coins, 63, 188
  college education reading, 12–13
  dreams, 188
  electricity, 188
  energetic match, 151–52
  on fear blocking pregnancy, 174–75
  feathers, 188
  on following gut, 20–21
  let it be, 10–11
  light flashes, 189–90
  music, 189
  on not trying to fix others, 139–40
  numbers, 26, 69–70, 189
  scents, 189
  on sickness from negative thinking, 46–47
  smudge spray, 84, 194
  on soul mates, 99–100
  on staying in or leaving relationship,
    144–45
  synchronicities, 13–14, 190
  on trust in unknown, 176–78
  on unhealthy friendships, 108–9
  wings, 190
  yellow roses, 118–19
Silencing, of feelings, 142–43
Silver cord, 85